MW00769617

Contemplative Enigmas

FR. DONALD HAGGERTY

Contemplative Enigmas

~

Insights and Aid on the
Path to Deeper Prayer

IGNATIUS PRESS   SAN FRANCISCO

Cover photograph
Monastery Cloister
Tama66/Pixabay

Cover design by Roxanne Mei Lum

© 2020 by Ignatius Press, San Francisco
All rights reserved
ISBN 978-1-62164-343-2 (PB)
ISBN 978-1-64229-105-6 (eBook)
Library of Congress Control Number 2019947887
Printed in the United States of America ∞

To John Haggerty (1958–2018)

Contents

Foreword

This book follows upon the heels of three striking volumes, *Contemplative Provocations* (2013), *The Contemplative Hunger* (2016), and *Conversion: Spiritual Insights into an Essential Encounter with God* (2017). Each of these volumes opens up a precious window into heeding Jesus' remark to his disciples at the outset of the Gospel of John. "Jesus turned, and saw them following, and said to them, 'What do you seek?' And they said to him, 'Rabbi' (which means Teacher), 'where are you staying?' He said to them, 'Come and see.' They came and saw where he was staying; and they stayed with him that day" (Jn 1:38–39).

Obviously the disciples were not simply asking about the location of Jesus' domicile. They wanted to dwell with him in a deeper way. Where Jesus himself dwells is "in the bosom of the Father" (Jn 1:18). He "became flesh and dwelt among us" (Jn 1:14); and we dwell with him when we perceive his dwelling with his Father. This perception comes through faith but, even more, through love. Jesus tells his disciples, "If a man loves me, he will keep my word, and my Father will love him, and we will come to him and make our home with him" (Jn 14:23). The Spirit enables us to perceive where Jesus dwells, "in the bosom of the father". The riches of God's own Trinitarian life are opened to us. Jesus says about the Holy Spirit: "he will take what is mine and declare it to you. All that the Father has is mine" (Jn 16:14-15).

The very identity of God is known when we know the love of the Father and the Son. In his Farewell Discourse, Jesus asks his Father to en-sure "that the love with which you have loved me may be in them [his disciples], and I in them" (Jn 17:26). This love is not far from us. It is simple: "If you love me, you will keep my commandments" (Jn 14:15). "This is my commandment, that you love one another as I have loved you. Greater love has no man than this, that a man lay down his life for his friends. You are my friends if you do what I command you" (Jn 15:12-14). When we love each other as Jesus loved us—with self-surrendering love —this is because the Holy Spirit "dwells with" us and is in us (Jn 14:17).

The contemplative asks to dwell with God. This same contemplative will also be the one who loves neighbors in need, God's poor. In the Gospel of Matthew, Jesus teaches in a parable that salvation will depend upon care for the poor. "Come, O blessed of my Father, inherit the kingdom prepared for you from the foundation of the world; for I was hungry and you gave me food, I was thirsty and you gave me drink, I was a stranger and you welcomed me, I was naked and you clothed me, I was sick and you visited me, I was in prison and you came to me" (Mt 25:34–35).

Reading *Contemplative Provocations*, I was gladdened that Father Haggerty urges contemplatives to "keep our eyes on Jesus of Nazareth".[1] This does not mean that we avoid experiencing God as hidden. But it instructs us about how to keep on the path. In his *Commentary on the Gospel of John*, Saint Thomas Aquinas observes that "contemplation is perfect when the one contemplating is led and raised to the height of the thing contemplated. Should he remain at a lower level, then no matter how high the things which he might contemplate, the contemplation would not be perfect."[2] The way to rise to a higher level is by grace, which enables us to adhere and assent by faith and love to

[1] Donald Haggerty, *Contemplative Provocations* (San Francisco: Ignatius Press, 2013), 31.

[2] St. Thomas Aquinas, *Commentary on the Gospel of John*, trans. Fabian Larcher, O.P., and James Weisheipl, O.P., ed. Daniel Keating and Matthew Levering, vol. 1: *Chapters 1–5* (Washington, D.C.: Catholic University of America Press, 2010), 4.

the triune God. This path will always be grounded in Jesus Christ.

In *Contemplative Provocations*, Father Haggerty warns that in contemplation we need to check our intellectual pretensions at the door. If faith in Jesus Christ overcame all mystery, there would be no self-surrender on our part, no love that patiently awaits the greater unveiling of the face of the beloved. In a time when the pope and cardinals were profoundly corrupt, Saint Catherine of Siena never ceased to cleave to Jesus Christ as the saving bridge. She did not waver in her faith that the Church was the body of Christ or that the priests were Christ's own. She begged for and received the gift of sight. "O abyss! O eternal Godhead! O deep sea! What more could you have given me than the gift of your very self?" "You, eternal Trinity, are a deep sea: The more I enter you, the more I discover, and the more I discover, the more I seek you. You are insatiable, you in whose depth the soul is sated yet remains always hungry for you, thirsty for you, eternal Trinity, longing to see you with the light in your light."[3]

In *Contemplative Provocations*, Father Haggerty assures us that "[t]he thirst of the soul for God is stronger in the desert."[4] He urges patience in fac-

[3] St. Catherine of Siena, *The Dialogue*, trans. Suzanne Noffke, O.P. (New York: Paulist Press, 1980), 364–65.

[4] Haggerty, *Contemplative Provocations*, 60.

ing periods of spiritual dryness in contemplative prayer. He speaks about contemplative prayer as a "poverty", as an awakening to our need for God in Christ.[5] Our love has to face its own poverty. "What God asks is that we accept the hard truth of actual poverty in itself, the emptiness in everything sought apart from him. It is always a certain desperation of need for God that draws his love in a deeper way."[6]

Here we find a jumping-off point that does not require us to be already a saint. We must admit our radical poverty and our yearning—which is the Holy Spirit's gift—for "the love of God in Christ Jesus our Lord" (Rom 8:39). Contemplative prayer, as a spiritual exercise, is not for the self-understood spiritual elite. We are to face our utter poverty and to find Christ therein.

Through his many years of working with Mother Teresa's Missionaries of Charity, Father Haggerty ensures that his invitation to us to face our spiritual poverty does not bypass the reality of economic poverty. He notes, "The appearance of real poverty is unmajestic, dirty, sometimes revolting. Nothing divine suggests itself."[7] Yet God shows himself in the poor to those who have eyes to see. Poverty is always an invitation to love. When we

[5] Ibid., 63.
[6] Ibid., 68.
[7] Ibid., 150.

turn away from the poor, we turn away from the truth about ourselves and from love. "The identification of Jesus with the poor man of all ages becomes a truth carved into every encounter we have with suffering. The poor man's thirst, in all its variations, is a perpetual reenactment of Jesus pronouncing again his thirst from the cross. Love or vinegar—these remain options until the end of time."[8]

In *The Contemplative Hunger*, Father Haggerty invites us to consider the seemingly desperate present-day situation of the Church from another angle. We tend to suppose that the future of the Church depends upon anything but real prayer. Father Haggerty tells us the opposite: "Contemplative life, even in its concealed quality, may be the most powerful adversary to the tides of secularization undermining religious belief in the modern time."[9] This is because real spiritual life pulses with a spiritual energy that people cannot ignore. We need to recall, "Every act of surrender to God of lasting spiritual value takes place in a silence deep within ourselves."[10] God is enough for us, if only we will surrender to him in the poverty of love. But this will mean, even in the Church, that we must be

[8] Ibid., 153.

[9] Donald Haggerty, *The Contemplative Hunger* (San Francisco: Ignatius Press, 2016), 29.

[10] Ibid., 124.

"willing to carry on along dark paths with no clear direction and with silent replies".[11] If we refuse to do this, our surrender is not yet real. Do we have "fire in the heart for the real mystery of God"?[12] If not, let us beg for it. Father Haggerty reminds us to be patient as we await an abiding experience of divine presence. Let us first allow "the reality of God on the Cross at Calvary to cause a great shock to our soul from which we never fully recover".[13]

In *Conversion: Spiritual Insights into an Essential Encounter with God*, Father Haggerty takes us farther along the path. He confronts us again with what Christianity is really about. It is about allowing God to be God for us, the opposite of our desperate wish for security and stability on our own terms. What God asks for is simple: "The choice for God".[14] Moreover, "God never exercises a last compelling push or shove across the threshold that finally takes a soul to its knees in a surrender of itself to God. There is always an interior act of consent to God that must be exercised deep in the soul."[15] Once made, the choice will continue to exert its power; the recollection of it has an impor-

---

[11] Ibid., 216–17.

[12] Ibid., 210.

[13] Ibid., 213.

[14] Donald Haggerty, *Conversion: Spiritual Insights into an Essential Encounter with God* (San Francisco: Ignatius Press, 2017), 24.

[15] Ibid.

tant role at all stages of our life. Yet, God invites us
to go deeper. We must enter deeply into the "crucified love" of God.[16] Those who follow this path
"will find that they cannot look at him anymore
without the wounds of his crucifixion before their
souls. The wounds begin to speak a language of
love in the silence of prayer. They beckon us to
offer ourselves for the sake of others, to surrender
in prayer to unknown costs, all out of love."[17]

No wonder that during Jesus' lifetime, people
demanded a sign of his authority; and how close
I feel to them! How close I feel to Peter, who,
even when Jesus had revealed his authority, "fell
down at Jesus' knees, saying, 'Depart from me, for
I am a sinful man, O Lord' " (Lk 5:8). Rather than
surrendering to self-surrendering love—no matter
how powerful such love might be—I am all too
eager to shield myself in my sinfulness and to urge
Jesus to try someone else. "From that time Jesus
began to show his disciples that he must go to
Jerusalem and suffer many things from the elders
and chief priests and scribes, and be killed, and on
the third day be raised. And Peter took him and
began to rebuke him, saying, 'God forbid, Lord!
This shall never happen to you' " (Mt 16:21–22).
How willing I am to cheer Peter on, lest I might
have to follow Jesus to the Cross myself! And yet,

[16] Ibid., 164.
[17] Ibid., 165.

I know that Jesus is true: the love of the Cross is the divine love, the path of life. So, what to do?

In the present book, *Contemplative Enigmas: Insights and Aid on the Path to Deeper Prayer*, Father Haggerty answers this question afresh. We must seek "a contemplative quality in life".[18] We will get nowhere until we see that "union with God demands a departure from self, a stark dying to self, an immolation of self, in order that a consuming love may deepen for our Beloved Lord."[19] This may sound harsh. In reality, of course, there is only the choice of either giving our lives to God or dying anyway and finding ourselves everlastingly handed over to God against our will, lacking love. "If any man would come after me, let him deny himself and take up his cross and follow me. For whoever would save his life will lose it, and whoever loses his life for my sake will find it" (Mt 16:24–25). "Enter by the narrow gate" (Mt 7:13).

What then? Again Father Haggerty presses us toward contemplative prayer, shaped by the cruciform pattern of love for others. Whether interiorly in the monastery or through life in the world, those who live a contemplative life of prayer must "go out boldly in search of souls, to win souls for Christ."[20] I cannot claim any great attainments,

[18] See below, 20.
[19] See below, 22.
[20] See below, 233.

either in prayer or in evangelizing. But Father Haggerty's books help people like me not to resign ourselves. It is time to lay aside "the active contest that takes place in the arena of egos".[21] It is time to "know nothing . . . except Jesus Christ and him crucified" (1 Cor 2:2). If this means knowing in prayer our own spiritual poverty, then all the better. It is along this path, in the interiority of our souls, that Christ crucified comes to meet us. Father Haggerty's counsel amounts to this: let us "take our knees to prayer".[22] Let us join God's poor—today.

—Matthew Levering

[21] See below, 239.
[22] See below, 256.

Introduction

> We are a spiritually impoverished generation; we
> search in all the places the Spirit ever flowed in
> the hope of finding water. And that is a valid im-
> pulse. For if the Spirit is living and never dies, he
> must still be present wherever he once was active
> forming human life and the work of human hands.
> Not in a trail of monuments, however, but in a se-
> cret, mysterious life. He is like a small but care-
> fully tended spark, ready to flare, glow, and burst
> into flame the moment he feels the first enkindling
> breath.
>
> —Saint Edith Stein
> (in Herbstrith, *Edith Stein*)

Contemplative life is generally little known, and
that has always been true in the Church. At least
in the past, it has been identified with the religious
choice to live in a monastic or cloistered separation
from the world. The monastic life of its nature has
an element of secrecy, hidden behind walls, apart
and distant from ordinary life. Perhaps by design,
the enclosure tends to encourage a forgetfulness
of these dedicated lives. And so not surprisingly

19

an aura of mystery surrounds the souls who disappear into silence and solitude and give themselves wholly to God, no longer to be seen. We have no opportunity to hear of their inner struggles, of their quality of love and sacrifice, or to ask if they ever arrive at their desired attainment of God and what that might be. Perhaps we look at them as privileged and elite souls, in their radical quest for God, or maybe we do not think of them at all.

On the other hand, there has been in recent times a healthy spiritual awareness that a contemplative quality in life is an absolute necessity if a serious pursuit of God is to be sustained over the long course of a life. A broader understanding has taken place. It is clear that the term "contemplative" itself cannot be confined exclusively to the context of a cloistered enclosure. More to the point, the desire for serious prayer has introduced many souls into greater depths of interiority in the spiritual life. Deeper prayer has awakened needs and questions. This phenomenon, interestingly, has taken place precisely at a time of crisis in the Church. The decades of internal conflict and crisis within the Church in the past half-century have been decades of a more intense turning to personal prayer—at least among some, for admittedly prayer does not capture the hearts of majorities. Indeed, this desire for deeper relations with God in prayer is clear evidence that Christ remains one with his Church through all times.

What, then, is the purpose of another book on contemplative issues affecting souls? People who acquire a serious taste for prayer do not realize initially the wonderful and *exacting* journey they have commenced in a commitment to prayer. Nor do they realize the effects and fruits it is bound to bring in time, not only to themselves, but to many others. It is the nature of prayer and deeper spiritual life that it radiates a light that stretches far in unknown ways. At the same time, there are unexpected difficulties, obstacles, and trials as we walk the long road of prayer. In that sense, prayer is like a marriage in which the love remains strong and unquestioned. The turns of life may entail at times wounds and sufferings, but they also deepen souls in their permanent bond. This is even much truer with God and a human soul. Every soul serious in its love for God undergoes experiences of testing it could not have anticipated beforehand, experiences often shared unknowingly in an invisible fraternity of souls passionate for God.

The title phrase of "contemplative enigmas" implies this confrontation to some degree with certain perplexities, confusions, and darkness in a long life of prayer. This is not simply a matter of riddles to be solved or puzzles to be deciphered, so that we can return to the comforts of prayer and no longer face difficulty. Serious prayer is inseparable from serious relations with God. An essential truth of divine love in its vast infinitude and utterly personal nature is its overpowering effect when a soul seeks God in wholehearted purity. There should be no surprise in this. Rather, we should expect that a life with God when pursued more than haphazardly will have demands of love that pale in comparison with all human relationships. And what is that primary demand of love? If we let God be in truth the God of infinite love, not trying to tamp down and restrict him in his fiery pursuit of our soul's complete offering, then perhaps we begin to perceive this challenge more intensely.

A precious thread of invitation weaves its way through the Gospel as an ultimate challenge; it likewise identifies the essential "conundrum" affecting all spiritual advancement—namely, losing ourselves in order to become transformed in God's love. "Whoever loses his life for my sake will find it" (Mt 16:25). The road to union with God demands a departure from self, a stark dying to self, an immolation of self, in order that a consuming love may deepen for our Beloved Lord. This never-concluded task of self-emptying is in the forefront of all contemplative pursuit of God. Indeed, all sanctity is tied to the surrender of ourselves unreservedly to God and his will for us. Interior prayer thrives or struggles inasmuch as we strive to give ourselves for the sake of others outside the times of prayer; and equally so as we live the same dynamic of a loss of self for the sake of love in prayer itself. Saint John of the Cross in an evocative stanza of his poem *The Spiritual Canticle* intimates the requirement for this interior transformation of the soul in love. His own commentary follows:

> If, then, I am no longer
> Seen or found on the common,
> You will say that I am lost;
> That, stricken by love,
> I lost myself, and was found.

> He who truly walks in love lets himself lose all things immediately in order to be found more attached to what he loves. . . . She became lost to herself by paying no attention to herself in anything, by concentrating on her Beloved and surrendering herself to Him freely and disinterestedly, with no desire to gain anything for herself. (*The Spiritual Canticle*, 29.10)

And what indeed, then, will be the actual experience of being lost while finding God as the Beloved? Many implications are buried in this image. The holy shroud that seems to wrap around contemplative life is unsuspected until its presence begins to be felt. This is not a death shroud covering a corpse but, rather, a veil of shadows enclosing the loving soul as it crosses into more serious depths with God. This spiritual darkness can seem like death to the soul that is not prepared or ready for it. As contemplative life advances, it pierces more deeply into the silent depths of a hidden God. It is *that* experience that can seem a slow dying within the soul, and in one sense it is precisely a kind of death. The presence of God in prayer can appear to be more an absence, and prayer itself an unbroken silence that God does not interrupt, in which he seems to disappear without leaving behind any trail. But in truth, God never departs or disappears at all. His presence is perhaps simply too close, too penetrating, and a soul has not adjusted yet to the shift in its intimacy with God. The experience of darkness is never all that is happening, and the good contemplative needs to realize another truth. The offering of a soul can become purer and more selfless in the shadows of this darkness. In darkness of soul, faith intensifies and love surrenders all its securities into the hands of a Beloved. The true spiritual path of losing ourselves in love for him, of disappearing from our own attention, of giving ourselves away completely, can flourish in earnest.

The effort in this book will be in part to address challenges, enigmas, difficulties of this sort that must be engaged in the life of more advanced prayer. Prayer is at heart an interior action of receptivity to God. We have to respond to invitations, take on inner dispositions, leap interiorly in uncertain directions in our quest for God. God summons us continually to the greater gift, and we must step forward in answer. Silent prayer before a hidden God has at times definite elements of trial. Certainly, it will display a mystery of varying intensities in our engagement with God's presence. But every contemplative soul knows as well how irreplaceable in life is the taste and knowledge of God's divine presence; and this truth, too, animates the reflections of this book. Each succeeding day of prayer can have its weight and glory, its uplift and seeming defeat. But beyond this daily pursuit, there are the signs of a divine predilection that mark a true contemplative intimacy with God. This book seeks not so much to unravel some harder dilemmas of spirituality but, rather, to expose the tracks and markings of this intimacy with God that are part of the intensifying path into a deeper contemplative seeking. Insights come often in spirituality as we pray with a sense of anticipation and receptive waiting. The book can be read in this spirit of contemplative expectation of insight.

One last remark might be made. There is a decisive moment in a spiritual life when we perceive that our life must be offered fully to God. And this is precisely an insight that may arise out of an experience of trial and darkness in prayer. The need for such an offering is a significant realization and presupposes a life that has been seeking Our Lord for some time. We might think that God takes care of this offering as long as we persevere in our fidelities, without a necessary part played by an additional decisive choice. But this may not be so. Perhaps it is necessary that we offer ourselves in a deliberate, concrete, conscious manner *to God*. We cannot predict the unknown consequences of what will occur afterward if we make this act the truth of our lives. Needless to say, we can expect, however, a great drive of desire to become henceforth more one with the heart of God. And who would resist this possibility if it beckoned before our eyes?

May all who seek God in deeper prayer discover that he has sought them and found them through all the hours of prayer. Their quest has been answered, even unbeknownst to them, in the heart of the hour itself.

I

A Leap of Self-Offering

I want to see you as a sacrifice of living love, which only then carries weight before me. . . . You must be destroyed in that secret depth where the human eye has never penetrated; then will I find in you a pleasing sacrifice, a holocaust full of sweetness and fragrance. And great will be your power for whomever you intercede.

> —Saint Faustina Kowalska,
> *Diary*

I feel that God leaves us free to choose between a measured love and a measureless one. But it would be a great misfortune to choose spiritual mediocrity—yet there is nothing but that or total immolation of oneself.

> —Raïssa Maritain,
> *Journal*

Those who in fact risk all for God will find that they have both lost all and gained all.

> —Saint Teresa of Avila,
> *The Book of Her Life*

If we ask what imparts greater love to a soul, what fire burns at its center, the reply must speak of an offering, the need of our soul to be poured out in an offering to God. The essential truth of love as an offering to a Beloved implies an endless quest during a lifetime. For there is always more to lay down and offer to God, until our dying breath. This desire at the heart of love to make a complete gift of ourselves is a response to Jesus Christ pouring himself out in a total immolation on the cross at Calvary. A certain threshold of contemplative love can be crossed only in tandem with the mystery of Jesus' Passion. We realize an ultimate truth of spirituality only in a deep longing to become one with the offering of a crucified Lord. "Love is nothing else but perfect self-oblation and abnegation, in order to give oneself completely to the loved one. Is this not a form of death?" (Hans Urs von Balthasar, The Way of the Cross*).*

Sacrifice, like the soul itself, has layers of secret depth. We should try in our prayer to enter inside these neglected layers, for they conceal intensities of love we may not suspect. In this inner realm of sacrifice, there are no limits or endpoints. The range of possibility extends far beyond sacrificial acts of a physical sort or the common self-denials of a day. Ascetical practices are a form of sacrifice, but they are never enough for a deeper spiritual life, and today, unfortunately, they are often ignored. They may strengthen spiritual discipline, but this is too narrow a view of sacrifice, missing its essential purpose. Self-denying mortifications can be managed simply by will power alone and lack love, without which sacrifice falsifies its name. What our *crucified* Lord Jesus would prefer from us is something more serious in love than the customary renunciations that are part of any good life. He wants sacrificial acts in the inner life that can unleash a fire within the undercurrents of our soul. He desires us to step over the edge, as it were, in offering ourselves to him in the privacy of interior prayer. He waits for bold, irreversible acts of surrender in prayer that cannot be taken back, like marriage vows, dissolvable only in death, yet repeated continually in life. Every intense sacrificial offering of this kind stretches love into the buried depths of the soul. These acts inflame our soul's passion for God; afterward, inevitably, they compel actions of generosity for others. The courage to place our future days at risk is their hardest demand, not knowing what God will do with the complete offering of ourselves to him. An almost foolhardy impulse to forsake our life at the hour we are surrendering it unreservedly becomes a necessity for a great love of God. All radical love for God may hide its deeper mystery within such private offerings made in the quiet of prayer. Unknown but to God himself, these acts pronounce a willingness to sacrifice everything for love of him as our beloved Lord and God.

~

It is not so difficult to perceive a spiritual hunger for these sacrificial acts of interior offering. The hunger for them can make itself known gradually as we seek God in what may have become a prolonged and barren searching in prayer. Over time the absence in prayer of a deeper enjoyment in the presence of God, the strain of seeking and not finding him, can carve an emptiness in the soul like a long bodily deprivation. The hunger will intensify in refusing to halt our commitment to silent prayer while apparently receiving little from prayer. At a point of frustration, at the edge perhaps of losing resolve, we can wait no longer. The yearning for his presence calls for a more extreme gesture in love, even if we are unsure at first what that might be. The thought of a more complete offering to God may then rise up out of the shadows of prayer, almost as a way to break a stalemate. It may be the distance from God we are suffering that attracts us to the deeper gift of ourselves to God. Indeed, a certainty may begin to be felt that Our Lord will be pleased if we offer ourselves in some great way, that he wants this gift and urges it, that Mary, too, wants it. And our hunger seems only to confirm this invitation. Surely it is best not to question, but simply to go forward, like a blind child holding out a gift and stepping ahead, unable to see who is waiting to receive this gift. The precise words of offering we may use are not so important. When the hunger is great, a soul manages always to express itself, and very likely the Virgin Mary will be there to assist. The words spoken, and the silence that lingers after them, will be placed into God's hands like precious stones ground into a shimmering dust and received into his divine heart.

∾

Private, sacrificial offerings of ourselves are in God's plan, desired by him, awaited by him. We know this truth inasmuch as we begin to experience over time a longing to give ourselves more fully to God. When these offerings are still in preparation, and not yet understood, they stir strong yearnings for God at unexpected moments, often unperceived, but more pronounced over time. It becomes clear after a while that this hunger for God must not be ignored. There are variations in how it shows itself. Sometimes a deeper yearning for God hides within the dry routine of daily prayer, almost distracting our prayer, a hunger dormant beneath emotion. More noticeably, it may pierce our heart suddenly when our eyes are closed after receiving Holy Communion and we want to say something to Our Lord and feel only tongue-tied. Another time the hunger may walk away with us like a restless companion at the end of an hour of prayer, not leaving us despite our turn to the day's affairs. Or we may experience this hunger for God in a strong desire not to leave prayer, to wait as long as possible before departing. It is unpredictable in its concealed ways, but one thing is certain. The presence of a secret invitation is evident in these symptoms. Perhaps Our Lord likes to see in us an almost desperate desire for himself, with no way to escape his pursuit. For this hunger as it intensifies plays a formidable part in the making of a soul. It introduces us to a passion for God that will overcome all rival desires. It is the serious impulse behind every deeper offering that will transform a soul permanently.

∼

Hunger sharpening its edges may carry us eventually to an inner crossroad where the only option would seem to be a leap into an uncertain abyss in the spiritual life. It is best then not to think too much or deliberate on what to do. An invitation is present that we cannot comprehend just yet. It ought to be accepted without asking for clarification or conditions. An unknown exchange with God awaits us with an unspoken promise of some deeper intimacy with him. Our soul cannot know yet what may come after offering itself up more fully, entirely, sacrificially to God alone. Let us recall that Mary likewise could not know how her own Yes at the Annunciation would alter her expectations of life. We should simply let the inner desire for this offering burn away all reluctance and hesitation. Concern for ourselves will diminish and even disappear when our desire is directed toward giving ourselves all to God. Nothing then will seem more important than belonging to him, being entirely at his disposal, stripped of needs that may have kept us too long at a safe distance from God. It is as if a threshold has already been crossed once we become aware that our yearning for God never leaves us, that it never ceases even when we are not conscious of it. Our soul needs to give an answer to that blessing.

~

When Mother Teresa in 1948 received permission to leave her congregation of the Irish Loreto sisters to begin her work with the poor in the slums of Calcutta, she wore for a short time a profession ring that had been given to her in Loreto when she pronounced her religious vows some years earlier in the former order. On that ring was engraved a phrase in Latin, which translated is "take all, give me souls." The ring soon disappeared from her finger, but the words did not. One of her sisters from the initial group to join her remarked that this short prayer became an ejaculation frequently recited by the sisters in their first convent. It became "our slogan", she said. And it was not a temporary prayer in the order. For years in the Missionaries of Charity, this phrase could be heard recited aloud in their convents as it was repeated in unison on Thursdays when the sisters did their weekly housecleaning. The words if taken seriously identify an essential task of a fully dedicated spiritual life— to offer all to God and let all be taken, so that by this offering, souls might be saved. Religious life in the past thrived in part because words such as these permeated lives in quiet, inspiring ways. There was a clear priority of purpose beyond bettering the world in a social sense. Ultimately the salvation of souls was at stake, and religious self-giving could contribute mysteriously and directly to helping souls arrive safely into eternal life.

In the early months of 1995, a young Missionary of Charity Sister contracted cerebral meningitis in Egypt. The immediate effect of this traumatic illness was to cause blindness. But in the first days of the sickness, when the Sister had been moved to their Cairo convent and was receiving treatment, it was not known yet whether the blindness was a permanent or temporary effect. The Sister caring for the blinded Sister proposed that the two should pray a novena together for the recovery of the Sis-

ter's eyesight. The Sister suggesting the novena was
confident that God would hear the prayer, and so
they must try. The Sister who had been blinded,
however, did not answer right away and then responded that she would not pray this novena, that
the other Sister could do so, but she would not.
She said that when she had taken her final solemn
vows in the congregation the previous May in Calcutta, she had told Jesus on that day that he must
feel free to do all he wanted with her, that there
were to be no limits in what he could ask of her.
"I prayed after receiving Holy Communion at that
profession Mass 'take all, but give me souls' and repeated it numerous times. And now I will not take
that prayer back. I'm sorry, but I cannot pray this
novena." Sometimes a person does take very seriously the implications of even a very short prayer.
And God, for his part, seems at times to take a person at his word, even when the words used are simple and few. This Sister never recovered her sight,
but from all I know of her, she has lived in a Calcutta convent these past two decades with a fearless
spirit of self-giving. One can have little doubt that
her small ejaculation has remained a large, piercing
truth of her life.

～

A prayer in which we offer ourselves completely
to God, placing everything in our lives entirely in

his hands, inviting him to do whatever he wants in our regard, may seem to take a great risk. But perhaps such a prayer is a necessity once we arrive at a certain plateau in our relations with Our Lord and seem to be moving nowhere. We need not wait for some notion of exalted holiness to embrace us before making this kind of offering. There is no requirement of steely detachment and indifference to the hard choices that might come our way in subsequent days. More than likely, we do experience some apprehension before such an act. The inner desire urging us toward an inner abandonment of ourselves simply calls for a decisive choice. Without realizing it, we have likely been longing for a release from the painful sense of holding back a gift from God that could be given. This kind of pure offering to God has really one demand: we must accept that God can now act freely with us, without consulting us, far beyond proposals we might present for our lives. We will learn in time that despite the seeming risk, God never takes advantage of generosity but, rather, brings the blessing of his presence in a new manner. He extends the reach of grace into our soul to match the depth of offering from our soul. What had been beyond our capacity to accept from God before such a prayer, even hard suffering, becomes possible to bear only because we have offered ourselves to Our Lord.

~

It is certain that with some souls God is quietly arousing over time a hunger for pure acts of offering to him. He draws a desire for these acts in a mysterious way never fully understood by a soul. They may not be recognized until we are virtually standing at the edge of them, ready to give voice to our love, yet not sure what to say. It can be that for a long time Our Lord inflames a yearning for himself that fills a deeper, unfelt aspect of prayer, and we cannot escape this yearning. An intense desire is present at times, a desire that we are unable to manage or control or even acknowledge with any clarity, but which works a silent effect in the hours of prayer. A strong, even overwhelming, hunger to meet God openly, no longer from a distance or from behind a closed door, as it were, but face to face, if such a thing were possible, begins to occupy one's prayer, almost interfering with it. The desire for a direct, immediate contact with God becomes a steady provocation in prayer, distracting and rattling our awareness. It may be a recurrent longing for an extended period of time. Then, without our observation, a change may seem to occur in the content of our desire. No longer do we desire some kind of direct contact with God that would leave nothing more to seek. Instead, our desire shifts to another possibility, and we experience nothing but a great yearning to offer ourselves in a pure act of love to God, to be taken up and offered completely to him. This yearning can

become a consuming obsession in prayer, much the
way we had been occupied previously with hunger
for a direct encounter with God. The desire for a
complete offering now absorbs our soul in prayer
and, often, outside prayer. In fact, it promises a ful-
fillment we cannot identify with any clear sense,
but which, unlike our former longing for a direct
contact with God, seems certain and attainable.

~

Let us be aware as well that it is only for so long
that we can remain in an indecisive state of waiting, unsure how to act, while bearing this deeper
hunger of soul. The scenario for acting would seem
to take different forms. Perhaps it becomes clear
to us on a certain day that our secure, steady sense
of prayer is gone. We cannot pray as our former
routines of prayer permitted. There is nothing familiar to hold onto or grip, nothing to lean on; no
thought of God provides support; no image brings
comfort. The hour is not planned for any definitive act of the soul, and yet the time may be propitious then to let go more deeply and abandon
ourselves into God's hands. The need for a pure
offering of ourselves can become a compelling desire in a single hour, unlike any desire in prayer
experienced in the past. This desire may hide itself inside a deeper place of interior yearning for

God, as though a flame were already alit within us prior to any definite act taking place. But then we must choose to act ourselves; our own choice must release itself toward the unseen presence of Our Lord's love. We may sense only later how real was his presence and his love in that hour. At the time, the purity of this offering to him is simply surrendered. We cannot realize in the hour itself what repercussions will come from a purer offering of ourselves. The uncertainty may indeed be a necessary condition for offering our soul more completely to God. No more than Mary could know at the Annunciation, we can never know how a deeper "yes" to God is received in his mystery or the manner in which our own soul receives his divine embrace. But not all is unknown: the leap into a new, uncertain interior terrain conveys a sense of being held in God's love in a very real manner. Inexplicably, without our examining it, we cross a threshold with these pure offerings, perhaps more so when the leap toward infinite divine love seems most reckless and risky.

∼

The possibility of "threshold acts" of this kind in silent prayer needs to be recognized. These acts, which always involve some interior sacrificial surrender to God, carry us by grace across boundaries into deeper layers of soul where a different intensity of prayer now becomes possible. It is as if by a more complete surrender to God we enter secret caverns within the soul. There a pure longing for God burns outside our direct control and is aflame even when we do not feel it. These inner caverns seem to be places within the soul of limitless desire for God. To the extent that nothing but God occupies our desire in these places of interior concealment, we disappear from ourselves. Our own concerns are forgotten. For some graced time, we can be empty of all desire other than a great hunger for God. We are concealed from sight and unaware of being concealed. This emptiness in wanting nothing but God becomes in itself a kind of sacred enclosure of hiddenness. Indeed, the emptiness felt in losing ourselves seems somehow one with a depth of hunger within the soul itself. This hunger ultimately has no witness except God himself. He seems to deny entrance to these interior caverns to all eyes, including our own. Once we are secretly in that hiding place, nothing matters but our desire for God, and nothing is needed to inflame this desire. It burns without direct perception, but the flame is quite certain. We realize its effect afterward when we return to the ordinary tasks of the day and sense a great mysterious hunger at the center of the current hour.

∿

The dilemma, after any time inside these interior caverns of more intense longing for God, may be how to find our way back. Since we enter blindly, without observation, we may wonder how to return again. There is no remembrance of a direction, no worn path, no recognized road; in fact, only a single point of entry may gain us access. The offering of ourselves to God in a serious act of surrender may be the essential key that unlocks the doorway. This act, when pure and intense, seems to carry us toward these hidden caverns within the soul. Sometimes the effect is immediate after a surrender to God; other times, there is a delay and an absence of knowledge. Nothing in the realm of serious prayer allows for easy predictions or planned results. What does seem true is that thresholds are crossed without our realization as we advance in *wanting nothing but God*. We are simply drawn to hidden depths in the soul when an intense desire for God permeates the silence of prayer. It is as though we were led blindly at those times into deeper yearnings for God and his love. The hunger that the soul experiences can be thought of later as a mere taste of what God himself possesses in his infinite mystery. In a very obscure manner, God seems to carry us inside these privileged hiding places for a brief brush of his favor. It is a mystery why one day and not another we are there, lost in him, with no desire but for him and for giving ourselves fully to him and his love for souls.

~

Not just any act of offering can carry us across thresholds to a more intense love for God. A great leap of soul must take place internally, a release from every sense of protected safety that holds us spiritually in a stationary place. All security in ourselves must give way, exchanged for a condition of risk. We have to let go and plunge toward God as though falling through air into the hands of another. The sense of falling and descent is not a collapse into helplessness; rather, we fall into firm, strong hands. In every deeper surrender to God, he clasps us closely to himself and takes us to a place of hidden repose within the soul that would otherwise be closed to us. We do not choose then where we find ourselves. It is never our determination or decision that leads or guides us. The destination, whether we are conveyed somewhere or remain still, reveals itself only mysteriously, and unpredictably, and afterward we do not know where we have been. We can only say we have been seized and held in a way known to God, who never informs us how this comes about. We realize only that a hidden place in the inner realm of the soul has concealed us for a time. And we know sometimes, too, a great longing for God that lingers and burns within these hidden depths of the soul.

~

"My beloved Lord, I offer my soul to you as your hiding place, your haven of concealment. Take possession of the depths that I cannot see or feel. Let the silence there be a place to rest your voice, let my dry longing be your comfort and welcome. I want to be altogether yours. I ask that you make my soul your own possession. I willingly offer it to you that you may occupy my soul permanently. Hide there, conceal yourself there, and let me carry you to others in that concealment. Speak to others in your voice with the words that I pronounce; speak as well in the silence that encloses my life. It matters not at all what fruits I perceive in the days to come as long as you are acting. I expect to see little; it is better that way. I have become accustomed to your preference in using me without my knowledge. Your action is more effective when your hiddenness remains. The more ignorant I am, the more you are present in fruitfulness" (a contemplative nun).

~

It can happen that the opportunity for a great offering to Our Lord coincides with a time of great personal pain. And who of us can say whether we are approaching such a day, when God's love for us, for instance, will entail a shocking loss of someone long close to us, a spouse or family member or even one's child. Unique to each life, that day may come with no preparation, not at all anticipated. A presence much loved is ripped away and disappears into the receding shadows, never to be returned. Recovery of life as lived before this day is not possible; all is altered. And yet this juncture in time, in God's vision and plan, is not for sadness and pain but, rather, invites a different understanding of God and, perhaps, a contemplative turn in life. Time is of course needed, but perhaps a single insight grants the light to perceive the truth of God's love in all matters of loss. A sacrificial act of offering must take place, more serious than any other renunciation we have made in our lives. It is a profound offering to God of what he has taken from us, holding back nothing, uniting ourselves now to his choice, even as this act may cost much in tears. "Yes, Lord, this, too, indeed everything you have asked, I offer to you." This act repeated possibly for many days subsequently may be decisive for all subsequent relations with God. The essential truth of sacrifice as an outpouring, a bloodletting of the heart, an immolation of soul, will reveal itself, and it must be recognized for what it truly is—an entry into the heart of God. All prayer, all sense of God's immediate presence in one's life, changes as a result. It can be why some souls discover a deeper intimacy with God only later in life, but when they do so, it is a profound shift in their awareness of the soul's relations with God in prayer.

~

"It is only the complete immolation of self that can be called love" (Saint Thérèse of Lisieux, *Sermon in a Sentence*). Whenever a serious offering of ourselves takes place in prayer—a single concentrated act can be enough—the repercussions and impact are bound to be felt. The same threshold act will become a need demanding to be repeated, a hunger that will return to our soul, sometimes deeply felt, leaving the traces and residue of a dissatisfaction with each offering made, as though each time it is never sufficient. The sense of finding a new intensity of love within our soul will be impossible to ignore. Yet, at the same time, the longing to love with intensity and give ourselves to others will goad us with a strange spiritual desire. The discovery of a greater frustration as love for God intensifies will urge repeated offerings, which are not possible simply by our own choosing. A time of waiting often becomes necessary, a delay that can weary and fatigue. A soul can suffer a torn and desperate quality, almost like a lover in the throes of confusion and peril, awaiting an answer to a declaration of love, convinced one hour of rejection

and the next hour of a joyful reciprocation of love.
The prospect of the former is often the stronger
and an anxious fear. The soul after offering itself
all to God can seem on the edge of collapse, about
to lose all. Actually, it draws ever closer to a decisive release stirring in the hidden depths of the
soul. It is perhaps only a matter of time before the
flames are known again to leap up and burn within
the soul. And always this will mean a desire for a
new offering in response to the divine surrender
that God now extends to the soul.

2

Thresholds in the Loss of Self

Since He Whom my soul loves is within me, why don't I find Him or experience Him? The reason is that He remains concealed and you do not also conceal yourself in order to encounter and experience Him. Anyone who is to find a hidden treasure must enter the hiding place secretly, and once he has discovered it, he will also be hidden just as the treasure is hidden.

> —Saint John of the Cross,
> *The Spiritual Canticle*

This absence of any return on oneself, this very pure desire of God alone, is the essential condition of contemplation.

> —Jacques and Raïssa Maritain,
> *Prayer and Intelligence*

To give oneself to God, recklessly forgetful of self, not to take account of one's own individual life to allow full room for divine life, this is the profound motive, the principle, and the end of religious life. The more perfectly this is carried out, so much the richer is the divine life that fills the soul.

> —Saint Edith Stein, *Thoughts*

The contemplative effort to lose ourselves in the presence of a Beloved is a necessity in prayer. Love, when it deepens in prayer, causes a detachment from self, an emptying of attention to self. Self-forgetfulness will always accompany a deeper experience of love for God in prayer. But this disposition of unconcern for self requires an effort at first. The renunciation of all desire but for God himself is a hard demand. This possibility of a pure desire for God determines the whole dynamic of prayer. Yet how difficult it can be to direct a pure longing for God alone and to seek nothing more from him than himself. There is here, too, a crossing of a threshold that we must seek each day in prayer by which we disappear and let God be all. Only then can our love for him be pure and selfless. "We can only go to the place where we are not yet. God only comes or goes to where he is already" (Elisabeth-Paule Labat, The Presence of God).

What "work" is initially taking place in contemplative prayer? We might say that if there is a "work", it is to cross thresholds of a sacred passage within the interior soul. No deeper encounter with God in prayer occurs unless we pass barriers that can obstruct and block us from the deeper mystery of God. And perhaps the most formidable barrier is the desire to take possession for ourselves of what can only be received as a gift from another. A renunciation of ourselves in prayer must occur, in part by relinquishing all desire for some "direct" experience of God. This desire to have an experience of God for our own satisfaction is common and understandable if we love him. But in letting go of the desire for a direct experience that we can savor for ourselves, we open ourselves to a more mysterious invitation. In contemplative prayer, thresholds in the soul are crossed blindly, unobserved by our own eyes, as we take our attention from ourselves and enter secretly into an interior hiding place. In that sense, there are no notes or instructions that might be used later for the same crossing. All takes place without a watchful eye, dependent on a release from ourselves. Once free from ourselves and our own desire to take possession of an experience of any sort, it is then that an encounter in love with the greater mystery of prayer may await us. Only a desire for God in prayer that refuses to glance back at self draws unnoticed favors in prayer. Often, perhaps, we do not realize this until afterward. What we do learn more over time is that a desire to surrender ourselves entirely to God draws us near these thresholds, takes us closer, and then, unknown to us, we are led blindly across them. Always there is the certainty of a gift completely beyond our effort or control.

$\sim$

Self-forgetfulness in prayer cannot be pursued as a deliberately cultivated attitude. We forget ourselves only as our attention no longer rests on self.

This occurrence has one primary requirement and condition. It happens when a deeper quality of love turns us in a purer manner toward God. It is only our interior longing for God that allows us to disappear from the sight of ourselves. A pure longing for God may even make the thought of ourselves cease entirely for a limited time. But this blessed unconcern for ourselves does not happen so easily in prayer, and we should ask Mary, who is the exemplar of selfless prayer, for her intercession. We are seeking a God who hides himself and his gaze from us. This concealment, in turn, makes it difficult to hide from self in prayer. Precisely when God seems most hidden, our attention is often thrown back painfully upon ourselves. In one sense, this tendency must be ruthlessly opposed. In another sense, it must be treated gently, by a calm turning in the direction of Our Lord in the tabernacle with the conviction that he is always in our company. Despite every false thought of his absence, he is close to us, waiting always for our heart's next expression of longing, whether in word or in silence.

～

"When I did not seek Him with self-love, He gave Himself to me without being sought" (Jacques Maritain, *The Degrees of Knowledge*). A place hid-

den in the heart of God awaits contemplatives as
they renounce any desire for status or privilege
with God and leave that ambition smoldering in
ashes. This renunciation has a significant consequence in the inner realms of silent prayer. The effect is to hide the soul more easily from itself. We
lose interest in self and have no need to gain anything for ourselves in prayer. Without a desire to
seek anything for self or to advance in some manner in our own estimation, a poverty takes hold in
us and becomes, as it were, an ordinary place for
prayer, less difficult to recover. We can return to
this poverty readily inasmuch as it attracts us, replacing any turn toward self-interest in prayer. We
learn then more often to discard at the doorstep of
prayer all traces of desire for an acquisition of any
kind in prayer. All desire to possess something for
ourselves fades and disappears. The desire for grat-
ification and favor from God becomes unnecessary, cast away as unimportant, no longer pursued.
The internal poverty may in time offer us a different treasure. There is now a new attraction within
our soul. We are beginning to know the drawing
power of the divine presence in the poor emptiness
of prayer. We do not perceive his presence in any
experience we can carry away as a memory from
prayer. It is confirmed more in the desires we take
with us from silent prayer to intercede for others
in spiritual need. It may be that the truest sign of

favor from God is a hidden union with his divine
thirst for souls. And this union we can indeed sense
more and more every day.

～

Who is *that* person favored by contemplative graces
in prayer? It is never, in one sense, the "I" we might
claim as our identity; rather, it is a hidden truth
within us, a hiding place where only those who
cannot see have access and gain entrance. There
our blindness is at rest under the gaze of God's infinitude, and we lose ourselves. The door is locked
to that hiding place if the ordinary "I" of our identity tries to enter. It is only opened from within
when this "I" disappears from view. We are drawn
into that hiding place in a blind way, with no remembrance of a path, leaving behind no trace of
steps. There is nothing in a path that we might remember in order to navigate our way once again.
And all this is because the divine gaze loves an inner depth of our soul concealed to the eyes that
would like to see for itself. It is known only to the
blind. We enter this hiding place within the soul
only in disappearing from view, vanishing from
ourselves as nothing and unimportant. What is enjoyed of God there cannot be carried back outside.
No possession is given in that hidden place of the
soul that might enhance the "I" of our identity and

become a possession and gain. On the contrary, we may realize in some confused and subtle manner how foolish and poor is every external claim of identity. Our true identity is that we belong to him, we are his possession, and that is all that is important. This most certain truth of belonging to him lingers within us, drawing us sometimes throughout a day, while he waits for our return in silent prayer.

~

It may seem at times in silent prayer that a barricade blocks us when perhaps it is only a thin veil. That veil may open gently for our passage once we renounce all desires for particular experiences. A necessary disappearance from ourselves can take place in forsaking all desire for the *possession* of a satisfaction in prayer. This renunciation, when it is decisive in attitude, is often the catalyst that releases our soul and opens that inner veil. And then we are carried blindly through a passage, without any need to see where we are taken. If, on the contrary, intent in our desire to get somewhere and to arrive at a target, we try to push forward instead of allowing ourselves to be led, and to force our way instead of waiting, we are blocked and impeded by our own desire. Almost every serious soul of prayer learns the hard lesson: there can be

no tearing through the thresholds of deeper prayer.
Delicate courtesy in the presence of the sacred is
an essential demand of contemplative graces. We
must wait patiently for the veils of grace in prayer
to open on their own, lifted by the divine hand of
love. Always this takes place in a secret manner, and
no soul perceives it except blindly. We learn that
we must wait, and then wait longer, not knowing
what day a different silence will permeate our soul
and the sacred presence in concealment will again
be near and inexplicably close.

~

"To reach satisfaction in all, desire its possession
in nothing" (Saint John of the Cross, *The Ascent of
Mount Carmel*). Contemplative love in prayer can
never be a matter of forceful effort or willful con-
quest. Love is required, of course, but the love in
this case is a gift that is received by surrendering
to it. Contemplative love has a single primary demand, which is that we wait receptively for someone already present within our soul to come to us
and be known. We have to wait for Our Lord to in-
vite our entry into a presence already hiding within
our soul. Always the rule must be honored that we
must wait to be received into his hiding place. We
are permitted inside only after his hand reaches out
to us and brings us inside. And it seems this oc-

curs by grace only as we disappear from ourselves in more intense longing for him and greater surrender to him. In losing ourselves, in giving up a self-consciously watchful manner, we are brought blindly to the desired place. When he takes our hand and leads us, as it were, we do not see where we are going or what we are crossing or the place where we have arrived. At the same time, the apparent simplicity and ease with which we receive his gracious hand can be deceiving, for this is not so easy at all. Waiting to be led can be a hard effort for a soul that longs for Our Lord and wants to possess him in love. We may prefer to take our own steps and grasp him by our own devices, to clutch at his hand when he seems in sight, and to make him draw and pull us toward him. The great patience required in contemplative graces is to give way and let ourselves be drawn by another's touch, especially as it is unfelt. Above all, we have to ask Mary for her motherly lesson in this delicacy of waiting in prayer.

∼

"[God] only comes to those who ask him to come; and he cannot refuse to come to those who implore him often and ardently" (Simone Weil, *Waiting for God*). A serious pursuit of prayer always has its own rules of engagement. For God can be like a

fire that leaves smoldering in ashes every attempt
to extract a satisfying knowledge of himself. Yet it
seems just as true that he has a particular love and
attachment for souls who seek him doggedly, im-
petuously, stubbornly, despite the frustration they
may inflict on themselves. A passion for God is
never without cost, but also never without some
return. The soul that does not halt in its quest for
God *does* receive gifts. But what is given as a gift is
never what is anticipated when we begin this quest
for God and, often, for a long time not recognized
as a gift at all. The waiting turns out in time to hide
his presence in a manner of more intense certitude
for the soul. The struggles of prayer give way to
the abiding recognition of a constant companionship.

~

The gift of knowing Our Lord's presence more
deeply in prayer can hardly be said to bring easy
comfort to the soul, or so it seems. In what may be
our more graced hours of prayer, we may seem to
resemble a blind man staring in the direction of an
unseen face we know is in the room with us, yet
do not see. An ambiance of darkness may be the
common encounter with the mystery of his hidden
presence. His presence reposes more often in obscure shadows, in grey mists, under dark clouds,

and these are understood after a time as a truer
knowledge of his presence than any exalted clarity
of thought or vision. For a soul of deep faith who
loves much, the mist and shadow hide an enor-
mity of presence, even as that truth is glimpsed
very partially. The conviction that God watches in
silence from behind a barrier of darkness can become strong on some days, undeniable, even overwhelming, and that conviction is enough even in
darkness. This is the singular gift granted the soul
that perseveres in its yearning for the eternal God.
The awareness is given that the presence of his gaze
rests on our soul as we stare back blindly at him. On
such days, nothing can shake the soul from the bold
conviction of his hidden presence: the certitude
comes from love. The recognition of his presence
may have no tangible sign of verification. Nonetheless, it is a knowledge indisputable and worth
every determined step in every long hour through
the strain of dark passages and empty silences.

~

In the great passage of the fifteenth chapter of Saint
John's Gospel on the vine and branches—"I am
the vine, you are the branches" (Jn 15:5)—Jesus
promised a pruning for those united with him on
the vine. The taste of hard struggle in prayer is
a symptom of this pruning and stripping down of

the soul. We should remember that this Gospel passage, recounting words of Jesus shortly before he left the Last Supper for Gethsemane, links pruning to the bearing of fruit. As an experience in prayer, the endurance of emptiness and unsatisfied desire does not convey any sense of spiritual fruitfulness. And yet a deeper recognition is possible. Fruitfulness in the spiritual life depends on the disappearance of egoism and concern for self. And bearing fruit will be impossible without a dying *within* ourselves, a loss of attention to self. A detachment from self is essential if we wish to walk this path toward the deeper personal mystery of God.

~

This death to ourselves in prayer ought in some manner to mirror our Lord's own self-emptying prayer in Gethsemane—"not my will, but yours, be done" (Lk 22:42)—and his prayer of abandonment at Calvary—"My God, my God, why have you forsaken me?" (Mk 15:34). Our prayer certainly does not experience the terrible dereliction of Our Lord in that hour of Calvary. Nonetheless, at times there can be a sense of futility tasted bitterly in prayer that must be abandoned to our Father's will. The emptiness conceals a more profound reality. In prayer we are united to a mystery of infinite proportions to the extent we accept an immolation of ourselves. When we cast away thought of ourselves and direct our attention to the nailed extremities of suffering in Christ's crucifixion, a fruitfulness is ready to be received mysteriously. We die to our own importance, and Jesus alone in his suffering is all that matters. Perhaps we never fully realize the power of his offering until we have become nothing to ourselves and seek him alone, which may require long hours of painful pruning in prayer over the course of many years. For it is absolutely true that we *are* nothing apart from him. Even Mary, despite her purity, came to know the intense truth of this nothingness of the soul. Prayer afflicted by a sense of weary futility is approaching a great truth if only we can turn a consuming attention to the beloved One who hangs fixed by nails on a Roman cross. That is a concentration and effort enough for any hour.

～

We have to sense perhaps at times in prayer a mysterious longing for God to reveal some unknown request to our soul. It is not like the ordinary longing for God sometimes felt, but a stir of quiet urgency to know some hidden summons that Our Lord seems to be faintly whispering, yet that remains unarticulated. We do not know *what* he is asking, but we sense *that* he is asking something

we cannot identify. Nothing is understood in any
clear manner, and yet we may sense a request hovering nearby, demanding attention, without arriving at a specific thought. It is like looking in the
face of someone who wants, it seems, to ask something, and yet nothing is spoken. Our prayer can
be seized for days on end by this sense of a question at hand that is still not heard. We cannot help,
perhaps, but repeat our own question—"What is
it you are asking of me?" The days may stretch on,
and still nothing steps out the shadows of silence.
The delay in receiving a reply may be part of the
answer. Indeed, the more serious a request from
God, the longer and more intense the waiting may
be. The desire to know may be inseparable from a
realization at a certain point that his most impor-
tunate requests hide within silence. The discovery
of his desire may then come as a surprise, arriving
when we are immersed in a deeper silence, with his
request no longer immediately on our mind. Even
without the help of words, and sometimes without
definite instruction, we know nonetheless a desire
to obey. And this submission will almost always
reveal his will to us with a greater clarity.

∿

By itself, the mind alone is never able to hear these
divine requests. We may strain our attention in an

effort to identify what is being asked, but we will get nowhere. These divine invitations require, on the contrary, a calm listening from a depth of silence within our soul, far beneath our mind. And that is why they do not easily reveal themselves. Only silence gives rise to their gradual emergence. Often this will mean hearing some words of Jesus in a new way. We realize that he is making an offering to us very personally. ''Do you want this? Will you give this to me? Will you accept this as my gift?'' Any one of these questions can shed a light on a current situation in our life. They may be pointing to an offering we have not perceived as necessary until that time in life. They stir us to extend ourselves beyond what we have given to God until then. They return a sharpened awareness of a quest that we must now pursue more intently.

∼

The ''threshold acts'' of sacrificial surrender to God while suffering darkness in prayer may lead to what can become in time a desire for a *pure act of love* in prayer. In fact, a pure act of love can be an endless quest in prayer once it becomes a desire in our soul, something never arrived at fully, and yet sought continually. We discover this possibility of a pure act of love through the trial and effort of prayer itself. For a time, perhaps, renunciations must be expressed and offerings articulated in words, our yearning to cast ourselves into the hands of God spoken in a clear act of language. But what comes later, as in all deeper love, is a release from any need to enunciate in words what we long for and, sometimes, an inability to use words. The purity of a deep love for God compensates for a loss of words and the incapacity of language. Great longings for Our Lord, at times underneath layers of soul, rise up from a silent place in the soul. We can only wonder if Mary's prayer was continuous in precisely such a manner.

～

The silent darker realms of enclosure within the soul seem to subdue our soul's inclination to speak, perhaps because they indeed hide the holy presence we wish to address. Words become unnecessary when the One we desire is present within us in a manner beyond the limited reach of words. A silent submission in love before his unseen presence becomes at that time the only need of prayer. This pure longing for God, while it remains, makes all need for language fade and disappear. Our capacity for speaking becomes not so much lost as simply left behind. In that short, unmeasured time, we have only one task, namely, to remain concealed with the One who is concealed within us. A hid-

den corner of the soul is all that matters inasmuch
as it has become a hiding place for encounter. Yet
this inner refuge we have entered is at best a temporary rest. The desire to remain there may be strong,
and we may be inclined to resist any return to ourselves. But always, regrettably, we must leave that
inner realm where a pure longing seems to come
easily, knowing that a return to ourselves is more
costly and painful each time.

~

Our human nothingness, mere dust before almighty
God, seems an inhospitable condition for a pure act
of love for God. The impression is unavoidable. It
is part of our soul's poverty to experience terrible
limits in prayer and the insufficiency of our love for
God. Yet perhaps no great act of love is ever possible unless our soul has become very poor, requiring a gift of love beyond our capacity. A painful
poverty must accompany every intense expression
of love. But it is also a dilemma if not understood
properly. The poverty might seem to contradict the
possibility for a pure love. We have to learn the lie
and deception behind that anxiety. For when God
finds a soul burnt and purified by its nothingness,
he smashes limits and stretches a longing for him
toward infinite vistas. It is he who loves then in
the soul even as the soul will seem to release an

act of love. This act of love takes place without the
soul's full awareness because it is primarily his act
within us. And he hides this love at times from the
soul's recognition. Such love is present in prayer
when we have become very silent and forgetful
of ourselves. Just as fire penetrates burning wood
when a wind fans it, so this act of love finds its
momentum beyond our soul's own power. It requires a kind of holy negligence toward ourselves;
no attention is given to self. And this may be the
real greatness of a pure act of love. It is no longer
simply our own soul exercising an interior act of
its own volition. In a sense, the soul has become
too poor for its own act. Someone else is present
within it compelling the offering of love. A mystery of love beyond our human capacity displays
its power. The favorable hour arrives largely to the
surprise of a startled soul. Or this mystery of love is
realized later in the day as a presence that seems to
enter the soul's awareness from elsewhere, without
being sought.

~

"An act of pure love is a very great thing. Oh, if you
understood that, you would not wish to learn anything else" (Sister Mary of the Holy Trinity, *Spiritual Legacy*). Perhaps a great interior poverty within
contemplatives makes them capable of a pure act

of love in prayer. After a while, they recognize this act as their one desire and their primary path to God. The desire for a pure act of love becomes in them an intense need because nothing else seems worthy of prayer. When a soul is naked and poor and wants nothing but God, the sole obstacle to its deeper love may be its own burnt desire for God. A flame still alive yet buried under ashes may seem to require constant stoking, but this effort is not required when souls are very poor. They need simply to disappear and forget their own crushed sense of constant longing for God. And perhaps God in his kindness favors these souls at unknown hours when they suffer most acutely from what seems a lack of love. God's desire for such souls shows itself at sudden moments like water bursting from an underground spring. The soul, without anything to give, needs then only to take no notice of itself. The divine presence gazing on the soul in love is the only truth that matters. Beneath a layer of desire that no soul can animate on its own, love draws the soul to a secret place of forgetfulness. Afterward, nothing but a return to this place of pure yearning for God can seem a proper aim of prayer.

∼

An act of pure love certainly exceeds a soul's capacity. Yet it can seem the exclusive demand of prayer when a soul has become very poor. But what can it mean to offer to God a sacrificial love that has no limits or bounds? Surely this act is desirable; yet it cannot simply happen and must be initiated beyond ourselves. In truth, only the eternal God knows in himself a limitless act of pure love. Nonetheless, he seems to place in contemplative hearts the yearning for a pure flame to burn within the soul for a time. If we cannot give to him as we desire, it must be that we can be vanquished by him in our desire. In the complete surrender of our desire to him, we may at times discover the secret to a pure desire to love. No such act can continue indefinitely as a perpetual inner flame, as it may have in Mary. Nonetheless, we can long at certain hours for a pure release of fire to flood the deeper layers of desire within our soul. On some rare days in prayer, this act may seem to wait for a spark to initiate it. Another flame may enter the regions of silent prayer and hover nearby, drawing our anticipation. And our soul may quietly sense that getting closer to this stronger flame will take us in a leap toward God himself. The prospect that God will act in that moment—a burst of fire reaching out to ignite a burning in our soul for him—becomes then the sole encompassing desire of our soul.

3

The Language of Silent Love

Silence has an authority all its own. . . . We must allow it to wash over us and enfold us. . . . We must be convinced that our many words are never better than God's silent emptiness in us. We must not, panic-stricken, begin at once to fill it with our own noise. God's silence in us is one of the choicest works of his grace.

> —Erasmo Leiva-Merikakis,
> *Fire of Mercy*

Only someone who is silent is listening. And only the invisible is transparent. To be sure, a deeper silence than mere abstention from speech and utterance is required. There is also interior speech which must also become mute, so things might find their proper utterance.

> —Josef Pieper,
> *A Brief Reader*

God alone can instruct you, you just have to give Him the time, and enough silence to hear a voice which makes less sound than a ray of light on water.

> —Jacques Maritain
> (in Barré, *Jacques and Raïssa*)

There is no prayer of a deeper contemplative encounter with God until a depth of silence within our soul becomes a consistent setting for prayer. Silence in prayer is the place of concealment for the hidden speech of God. We discover over time that the presence of God hides within layers of silence in our soul. The silence itself is not God, but it conveys a language that God speaks without words. In silence, his presence draws us mysteriously and becomes an invitation to long for him. It is not necessary to receive words of a message from God. God speaks a single word simply of his presence in love. We know it when our own desire for him has once again been inflamed with longing. The silence itself then disappears from our attention, and his presence of love is the only truth for the moment. "To be capable of receiving much from God, that is the whole of perfection" (Raïssa Maritain, Raïssa's Journal).

Among people of faith, it may be that very few seek a deep quality of inner silence in their prayer. Yet prayer can have no significant depth without this inner silence. There is a necessity in prayer to listen to Someone beyond ourselves, and often to listen to *his* silence, and this is a hard discipline. Listening to God requires an attentiveness in silence not at all easy to achieve. Our attention must be directed toward Someone present besides ourselves in a setting of silence and solitude, someone else whose presence captivates our desire even when he does not speak. Faith is of course needed to know this Other who is present and yet not seen. Contact with that Other who is God himself always demands a turning away from interest in ourselves. And many people, when they have some silence in their prayer, become conscious primarily of themselves and never lift their head up, as it were, in the direction of another presence. They may be accustomed to fill silence with thoughts wrapped around themselves and personal needs, a habit detrimental to prayer. The possibility of an encounter with God in silence, however, requires a capacity for remaining quiet before the invisible presence of another. A turning away from self, even ruthlessly, must often be a deliberate choice at the start of silent prayer. On many days, this first effort to focus our attention on God is a difficult exercise. The attentiveness to God in silence will be hard or even impossible until a steady concealment from ourselves in prayer becomes more habitual.

$\sim$

If calm is needed for thinking, silence is needed for love. This is an indispensable truth in our relations with God. There is an absolute necessity in prayer to listen within our soul to the voice of another. We can do that only through the habit of entering into an *attentive* silence in prayer. His divine voice speaks, not so much in silence, but by means of silence, for this is precisely his language. That is not to say that in our interior silence, he will speak words that we comprehend. No, the silence itself is his speech and his language. If we seem to comprehend words of any sort, the intermediary of a translation is likely at work. God prefers, it seems, not to speak particular words so directly but, rather, to speak in a language of desire that enters the silent, hidden realms of our soul. Perhaps the idea of silent speech, of speaking without words, seems incompatible with the nature of language. The paradox of a language of silence is nonetheless beyond dispute for those experienced in prayer. The fact that silence is not an obstacle to communication is one of the important discoveries made in our prayer. It is indeed God's primary way of communicating: in silence, he speaks a wordless communication of his presence. This presence in silence is heard in the way that a faint, indecipherable sound can be heard rustling the grass in an open field, when we do not know what we are hearing. In a similar way, the presence of someone approaching can be known without the person yet coming into sight. The sound of the approaching presence is dimly recognized; but nothing is seen, and no voice is heard. The silence we experience in prayer conveys this same sense of presence while keeping concealed the one who is communicating. He is never in any vivid manner observed, yet he makes himself known in this silence. No face is seen, and no encounter with actual words occurs. The silence of his definite presence is the single stark reality. In the midst of it, in the very silence itself, his concealment speaks his presence. But even in hiding, it is a presence alive and utterly real.

∼

Solitude needs silence, and a silence toward ourselves, if we want to be instructed by God. Silence brings, as it were, a vertical perspective into solitude, beckoning us to listen underneath the surfaces of life. It invites us to plunge inside hidden depths within our soul. Spiritual truths open themselves to being gazed on and "touched" in this silence. Perhaps God allows himself to be in a certain sense touched momentarily in silence, a blind touch on our part since we are unable to know fully what has been encountered, but nonetheless a contact with God. It is silence that makes this encounter possible. The truths of religious faith engaged without silent reflection, however, are often superficially met. These truths may remain simply abstractions siphoned off the pages of books until we allow silence to bring them to life in the solitude of our soul. The words of Jesus from the Gospel, in particular, can become vibrant and piercing in silence, speaking as though from a passage of eternity into the immediate hour. Indeed, silence when we are alone draws out our capacity to hear eternity in a word of Our Lord. We do not realize perhaps that we possess this understanding until we experience it. Then we can ponder the true significance of God as a presence speaking in the current hour. He instructs in the silence itself, by means of the silence, by words hovering in silence as though they were entering into time from eternity just at this hour. He casts light on the hour of silence itself, granting to our solitude whatever we need perhaps to hear from him. The silence, when it draws us to nothing but listening, is a sign of his companionship in the solitude.

~

Salvaging the mind's natural capacity for intelligence has become an essential spiritual task today if we are to take prayer seriously. And it faces stiff challenges. The first challenge may be the deleterious effects of dependency on technological distraction. The use of technological devices has become so ubiquitous in lives that it would seem almost perverse and "unnatural" to imagine a human life deprived of them. But what is the actual repercussion of this phenomenon? The contagion of perpetual distraction had swept into the mental lives of people to a degree unprecedented in history. Whereas in former times, distraction was a common difficulty in the struggle to give full concentration to prayer or work, now it has become a kind of "companion presence" in many lives. It is not an intermittent obstacle, but constant in its consuming pull. Most people surely do not recognize their habits of impulsivity in turning to technological devices for some form of distraction. It is as though a compulsive need for distraction had become a new drug-resistant disease of the mind, and nothing could tame or halt it. But it must be confronted as an impediment to spirituality for anyone interested at all in a deeper relationship with God. An *empty* silence without the noise of obsessive distraction has always been a requirement of prayer. One can guess that no one mentally slavish to a smart phone or a computer screen can have much patience for the attentive silence that alone can foster a deeper life of prayer.

~

"Man is becoming a technological object while vanishing to an ever greater degree as a human subject, and he has only himself to blame" (Joseph Ratzinger, *Introduction to Christianity*). A life uncomfortable with silence perhaps cannot remain long without some form of mild aggression against silence. Today the "weapons of technology" are the common antagonists to interior silence, and they perform their task quite well. Naturally we do not perceive technological gadgetry as elements of aggression in the spiritual life, and often they are not. Communication and access to information depend on them; the workplace would shut down without them. They assume, however, an aggressive mode when outside of work they preoccupy our mind to excess, insisting on attention, demanding to be used. All the while a kind of subtle resistance is directed against the spiritual need to calm down in silence and detach a bit from technological stimuli. A desire for some silence is often treated as an abnormal inclination, a tendency at odds with living in today's highly electrified world. In truth, the aggression implicit in compulsive technological use is directed, not against silence in itself, but against an emptiness of soul. In a soul cut off from God, a naked gaze into the abyss of self must be avoided at all cost.

∼

The compulsive use of technological devices always involves to some degree a separation from the concrete immediacy of actual reality. Virtual realities on a screen or held in a hand replace encounters with real objects and real people. Those who rely on technological devices throughout the hours of a day may argue the opposite. They may say that communication is the pretext and rationale for the use of technology. But with our eyes fixed on a computer screen or a smartphone, we may often indulge ourselves at whim, exploring a private world of labyrinthine self-interest, feeding an insatiable drive for diversion and useless information, or simply satisfying a need for some artificial semblance of human contact. Shutting down technology at intervals in order to remain silent and alone is essential if we are to think with lucidity and deeper spiritual insight. Training ourselves in a taste for the silent hour in solitude—*sans* technology but for the light of a lamp—must become a cultivated choice. Is it exaggerated to suggest that a survival of any sense of an immortal soul within us may be at stake? The danger is quite real that souls habituated to constant technological stimuli will never be silent with themselves, never alone in a receptive manner, and so never able to discover God in a personal encounter of prayer.

∼

A primary reason for the difficulty of listening in prayer, besides a tendency to focus on ourselves or the overuse of technology, is a subtle orientation present in prayer that must be conquered. What we initially may hope for in prayer is some experience, some feeling of satisfaction or delight that will confirm the value of prayer, and this, too, must be renounced. The demand of prayer is more basic, certainly harder, and perhaps not recognized. Ideally, prayer is for a time of quiet, a time without sound and noise, in which no word of our own is needed. We want an interior silence that can be interrupted by the word of another, who indeed can speak without words. The presence of God in itself can become a form of communication. The paradox of God speaking without words in silence is undeniable to all who experience deeper prayer. It can only be explained by referring to a different form of communication, a new language that must be learned. This silent language is a reality to those who have experienced it. The pattern is steady and recurrent by which this communication takes place. It is as though our longing for Our Lord in silence draws him out from a hiding place within our own heart. There he is encountered to our surprise, and yet it is not so surprising, for this occurs precisely when we are longing in silence for him. The longing of our soul seems to be a call to him in some personal manner, but a call from deep within our heart, without particular words. And then he is suddenly known to be present, even as we remain blind, without sight of him. In that longing, the certitude of his presence can be strong, even if it is not felt in any direct manner. This sense of his presence in silence may be difficult at first to accept until we realize how real his communication is. But when this manner of communication happens more than a few times, it is unmistakable. Some might say that an idiosyncratic conviction is at work, but this is not so. His presence in silence is accompanied by a deep certitude that someone speaks in that silence in the depth of the soul. No particular voice is heard, no words are enunciated, but the communication nonetheless takes place. It has only to be believed to become irrefutable to the soul. One immediate effect on the soul is a profound respect for the sacredness of silence. We want more of it then in our lives because God leaves some trace of his touch in that silence.

~

To accept that in prayer God speaks in a foreign language can be disconcerting, especially if until that time we have assumed that the words we were using were satisfactory. In fact, this assumption may be quite incorrect. God's preference may be otherwise. He may desire that we learn *his* language, a language, not of words, but of a communication of silent longing within the depth of the soul. This is a difficult language until we discover that words and

grammar are not the essential requirement in this
language. Actually, we have already some awareness of a language of silent longing in the experience of a deeper love for any human person in our
lives. The need of words can be dispensed with
when love is strong. And God certainly does not
require words when he wishes to communicate his
longing of love to our soul. Nor does he require
that we speak particular words in prayer to make
ourselves known to him. His way of speaking in
prayer is through the longings we experience for
him. Without words and in a silence that can permeate even the corners of our soul, he draws us
to his personal presence. His presence is known
as he provokes desire when we are absorbed in
a deeper silence within our soul. Our awareness
is not directed toward ourselves, then, but carried
by a longing toward him. A real communication
takes place as we turn toward him by means of
this longing. Like all languages, this one, too, displays levels of advancement. It is a language that
acquires much beauty and subtlety when it penetrates the inner layers and crevices of the soul. In
these deeper regions of the soul, a more intense
longing for God can be experienced at times even
as an absence of God. The desire for his presence,
strong and unrelieved, burns like a flame fed by
some hidden source. The sense of absence seems
in itself a form of communication of divine love

to the soul, which can make this a confusing language. Who at first will realize that communications of his hiddenness can advance a soul in the longing of love? A soul needs perseverance in faith to awaken to this truth.

~

Does knowledge of truth require language, an incorporation in linguistic expression? The use of language may be an ordinary means to the understanding of any truth. But is it correct to say that we know truth only inasmuch as we can enclose it in precise words? Does the communication of the truth of love depend on verbal articulation? Or is there not an experience as well of the truth of love in a stark silence that resists enclosure and containment in language? A truth that remains inviolate and sacred while submerged in a condition of silence? Clearly love can speak to the heart in unquestionable certitudes that need no further linguistic analysis. The silence in the midst of which God meets our interior spirit in prayer is ideally an inarticulate, wordless encounter of mutual love. This silence makes no argument for God's presence; there is no need for an explanation. It often speaks no clear instruction, commands nothing definite, leaves no buried message to be later dug up and interpreted. The truth of the encounter with

God in silence lies outside a formulation of language. It is conveyed without words, underneath layers of silence, in a sacred stillness. The communication is an exchange of wordless desire in love, a taste within desire that even without articulation conveys the certainty that God alone is desirable. The heart knows it has been drawn by love to a desire beyond its own capacity, and this in itself is a sufficient communication for any day.

～

On certain days in prayer, it may be that the desires of Jesus on the cross are speaking, and we must listen. To hear his heart's desires at his crucifixion, we have to remain very quiet ourselves, attentive to his silence on the cross rather than to the sound of a voice. The shouts around him, the noise of cruel brutality, are a disturbing obstacle, but we should ignore this. If we are to hear better, our inner eye must open and his battered face must occupy our attention, his struggle to breathe, his fitful movements on the cross. His body's agony is not silent if we listen with care, and his heart can speak to us. In three hours on the cross, he spoke few audible words, yet his divine yearning stretched out toward vast multitudes far beyond Calvary. All history with its passage of souls passed through his human heart. In silence we can be aware of his entry into countless inhospitable hearts that to this day resent his presence near them. We must accept for ourselves as well his torment in being treated as an unwelcome intrusion. What may seem hard hours in our own prayer on certain days perhaps conceal a mystery of encounters with unknown souls in grave need, souls who must be prayed for. Jesus cried out his thirst for these souls while hanging on the cross, a thirst that does not cease in heaven. It is satiated whenever a soul returns to his mercy, and for this we must pray in every current hour of prayer. In those times of prayer in a silence in which we care for nothing but his painful thirst for souls, our own need matters little. Our own small sufferings disappear in the dust stirring near the cross. In looking up, nothing keeps us from hearing his cry of thirst for the lost souls of the present day. Whenever we do hear these words again, we should leave prayer urgent in our own desire to spend our lives for souls in need.

~

A private exchange with God without words, in a language of longing, is secretly enjoyed in all contemplative life. There is no contemplative life unless wordless communications take place between God and a soul. Often a soul is not very aware of how deep this exchange is until silent prayer is concluded. But a further demand of love is always present if we receive anything in love from God. The contemplative exchange with God has its own exigency. Prayer of this sort must empty and purge the soul, so that the soul is stripped of possessiveness toward everything it might claim as a spiritual possession. If the prayer is not self-emptying, if it does lead to a forgetfulness of ourselves, something necessary has not occurred. The exchange has been one-sided and has not been completed. A misappropriation has taken place in what has rather to be given away. We hold on possessively to something that does not belong to us. There is perhaps a corrective to that. Every real contemplative encounter with God must linger after prayer as a quiet longing to belong only to God. In that sense, the desire for him must carry on long after we have left a time of prayer and continue like the echo of monastery bells fading into the distant silence. It is as though they were not ending as a sound, but only moving farther on into the distance. So, too, the desire to remain attentive to him and his will does not stop drawing the soul but, rather, carries on into the day.

~

Eloquence has little attraction for contemplative souls. On the contrary, the tendency of every form of deeper prayer is to draw language to a purer simplicity. A few words are enough to convey a soul's passion for God. Often these may be yesterday's words. The repetition means nothing; novelty is unnecessary. Each day the encounter with the divine presence is new; nothing said previously inhibits the freshness of the current hour of prayer. In this regard, we have to distinguish what God seeks in relations with us, which may be different from our needs in human interactions. On any day we may have to bear a certain boredom as a human experience when a conversation is dull or struggling. But boredom is not a temptation for God when he gazes on a soul with great loving desire for him, no matter how tongue-tied the soul has become. The inability to speak worthy phrases is no barrier to his love. He does not ask for poetry or fine language. More than beautiful words, he may desire from us the eloquent incapacity for speech, a silence that can only long for him without the benefit of words. Perhaps he is able to reach more deeply into our soul with a more piercing gaze when we are incapable of words. In these hours, his thirst to give himself arrives without interference to the silent depth of our soul.

～

Words in prayer may at times fade quickly into emptiness as soon as they are released. Nothing may seem to remain of them in the dry silence of a strained hour. But the truth is different. For the longing for God concealed in these forgotten words crosses an interior chasm where another silence now meets them. In the quiet of prayer now, there is no reason for us to bruise the silence with further words. The silence itself now soaks these words with an import beyond their simplicity. We do not need inspired language in speaking to God, only a serious desire for God within the soul, which we often may not realize is present. A deep longing for God transforms the simplest words into a language of love. Indeed, sometimes a threadbare phrase, even a single, weary word, is enough to ignite the unseen flame. The small word from our heart can turn from a flame to a fire when we are silent to every other desire and yearn for the Beloved. The only way perhaps to know this truth in prayer is to remain silent after speaking, forgetting all else, not looking to say more. After the words, there is nothing more to desire, nothing else to anticipate, but his silence meeting our own.

∾

Silence in prayer becomes for the one who prays a form of poverty. In fact, the silence in prayer must make our soul poor if it is to be a setting for an encounter with the hidden presence of God. Silence as a form of poverty in prayer is due to the longing for God that can accompany silence to an intense degree. Our longing for his presence in silence does not lead necessarily to a sense of encounter. The silence allows us to be receptive, it fosters attention, it provokes yearning, but it does not in itself convey the presence that is desired. Other factors and contingencies are at work, and grace must intervene. God is not subject simply to our desire, as strong as that may be; he is not compelled by our desire to show himself. It seems, rather, that he prefers more often to surprise us in prayer after our longing for him has stretched our soul for some time. We are usually not expecting those times when we are granted some experience of an encounter with him in silence. It is almost always not so clearly anticipated. If we wonder about this, an observation is possible. He seeks souls that search for him with wholehearted desire, souls upon whom he can take special interest, and he is not outdone in the earnestness of this pursuit. But neither does he give up his hiding place so easily. He is the one who takes the lead in relations with himself. Always he is a step ahead, and sometimes we are left behind and need to catch up. Many people will acknowledge that the hiding of God in silence can seem at times unyielding and heartless, but this is perhaps just a sign of love's pain in pursuit of a Beloved. Other times there may be no sense of a hiding at all, but that reprieve, as it were, never lasts very long. His silent presence must be loved with a great longing most especially when he is in hiding. That, indeed, is the only answer to his concealment—a blind man's longing to know the touch of the one who is loved. The darkness that surrounds a man who cannot see may stir profound longings within his heart when he is aware of the presence of a loved one close by in the same room. The inner spirit of our soul in prayer must come to know this desire of a blind man sensing a silent presence in the darkness. We, too, must grow in a capacity for a love that is beyond our power to see.

∼

"The one who is truly resolved is silent. It is not as if being resolute were one thing and being silent another. No. To be resolute means to be silent; for silence alone is the measure of power to act" (Søren Kierkegaard, *Provocations*). If there were no need for silence in prayer, there might not be any reception of a silent request from God outside prayer. Our soul must know that a silence resides at the heart of existence, and yet actual real life seems to display the opposite truth, with all its incessant noise. Nonetheless, a mystery of silence never disappears, never gives up its life. The hum of noise at all hours in a city only conceals this silence. It is true, by all appearances, that the turbulent noise can seem an aggressive antagonist to silence, its raging conqueror, a tyrant locking silence away in an unreachable location. A frustration inhabits any life that permits the crushing of its deeper needs. Yet how few lives really understand. Only those serious about prayer, who give some extended silence to each day, are capable of this testimony. They know by silence an inner truth residing in mystery not only in their soul itself, but in reality, despite the surrounding decibels of frustrating noise. There is no need for a hard exercise in this effort, just commitment at first, and then cultivation of an acquired taste. Silence in itself, when the mind and spirit are accustomed to quiet and listening, manages to instruct always with an attractive power. It is God who is a teacher in the silence, instructing, not by lecture and explanations, but in a manner of wordless impact and fluency. But we must attend to him and his silence with consistency to understand the way of this teacher.

4

The Thirsting Effort of Prayer

By its very essence, love is only thirst for love. . . .
The missed opportunity is the one that counts.
Tenderness through prison walls: this is perhaps
the greatest tenderness. Prayer is fruitful to the extent that God does not answer it. And sharp stones
and thorns are what nourishes love.

> —Antoine de Saint-Exupéry
>   (Leiva-Merikakis, *Fire of Mercy*)

In prayer, we have first to experience the dissatisfaction of our own desire, confess our own lack
and recognize in faith the absent presence of God.
This should lead us to desire the desire of God
Himself, that is, to desire what God desires and to
let God desire in us.

> —Jean-Claude Sagne
>   (in Congar, *I Believe in the
>   Holy Spirit*)

Until this possession, the soul is like an empty ves-
sel waiting to be filled, or a hungry person craving

for food, or someone sick moaning for health, or like one suspended in the air with nothing to lean on. Such is the truly loving heart.

—Saint John of the Cross,
The Spiritual Canticle

The sacred encounter of prayer demands the cultivation of interior dispositions, for it is a serious matter to seek God. We have to leave aside our usual preoccupations and enter a realm of depth in faith. Entering into silence requires a great receptivity to God in his hidden mystery. Indeed, an hour of prayer is often affected by what we do in the first minutes of prayer. Turning ourselves in the direction of God in a pure manner is an effort that has inevitable difficulties and obstacles. We must confront the concealment of God, without interpreting it wrongly. We must face the unpredictable retreats and withdrawal of his elusive presence. We must maintain our pursuit earnestly while realizing at times that we find him in the search itself. In all of this, hiddenly, he seeks to draw our soul's offering and love. "My longing for truth was a prayer in itself" (Saint Edith Stein; in Posselt, Edith Stein*).*

"Scrape away the soil and a spring will gush forth" (The Virgin Mary at Lourdes to Saint Bernadette). Mary's words are a helpful image for the initial effort of prayer. But what in prayer is meant by scraping the soil, the cover of ground and dirt that keeps the concealed spring from releasing itself? At first

glance, perhaps, the image suggests the need to remove the heavy burden of sin, so that the living water of grace will flow. But it may identify a more
fundamental necessity as we turn to God in any
silent hour of prayer. The exterior egoism of our
lives—in another image, that strong jetty of rocks
jutting out into the sea, with its crashing waves—
must allow itself to be overcome. The customary
center of our lives must disappear from view, as
those rocks disappear when submerged in the rising tide of the sea. An act of renunciation is needed,
a scraping away and a letting go. An entry into the
silent presence of the Almighty Lord demands that
we leave our concerns to some extent behind us
and outside the door of prayer. Renunciation of our
external self is required as a preliminary act. This
is not just the person of activities in the world.
An external personality is unavoidable in life. Yet
there is something always provisional and unreal in
our usual sense of self. It ordinarily narrows us and
constricts our interior passage into spiritual depth.
It blocks the flow of any spring from within us.
It needs to be released as we enter the sacred encounter of prayer.

∽

What to do, then, at the beginning of prayer? Fighting the temptation to turn our thoughts back on

ourselves in the early silence of prayer requires a mental discipline. Otherwise, the presence of Someone beyond ourselves, close in his gaze and listening, may be ignored and missed. As we begin prayer, he waits on the other side of an invisible veil of silence. And who will open that veil for us? We approach nearer to it only by a pathway of silence within our heart and mind. It is not a long passage, in no way a steep climb, but rather like a descent down a wooded incline into a silence where the trees, as it were, open in front of us once we are near them. No deeper contact with Our Lord takes place without this walk into an interior silence. The first effort demands a recognition of a real presence that draws our desire to silence. Our soul must turn in faith toward the One who cannot be seen, trying to rest in the certitude that he awaits us. It is like a traveler taking a quick glance into the distance before beginning his descent into a valley wrapped in a morning's silence. Once we realize again that we are seeking someone who awaits our approach, we can listen for his welcome. It is no longer then just ourselves moving in the direction of a destination. The path toward him is also the path that awaits his arrival. And then on occasion he may surprise us in the silence with a strong sense in faith of the opening of a veil and the immediacy of his presence in the near proximity of a tabernacle.

~

In the first moments of prayer, an act of silent adoration toward God—slowly, profoundly, even in making the Sign of the Cross—places our awareness in the mysterious presence of God. The presence of Our Lord in a tabernacle or monstrance calls for such an act. That initial contact with the divine presence demands a humble step in truth. We prostrate our inner spirit before the gaze of a God who looks at us in Jesus Christ with human eyes and yet stands in front of us from the infinite distance that separates his love from our own. There is a chasm of an immeasurable mystery in this encounter between a mere soul and God himself. We do not lift ourselves across this incalculable distance. We can only plunge by loving adoration toward his mysterious presence. All the while, a very personal gaze rests on us and reaches out to lift us past a barrier that is within us. On certain days, a release inside our own heart can take place, and then we are in a hiding place where there is no holding onto anything, no clinging, no concern for self. Our awareness can give up any particular focus, and we are hidden from ourselves, a blessed forgetfulness replaced by captivation with the gaze of another. We become for a time like a jetty submerged in the ocean waves that now cover it at high tide.

∼

"All difficulties in prayer can be traced to one cause: praying as if God were absent" (Saint Teresa of Avila, in *The Thomas Keating Reader*). This "absence" of God in our prayer, or, more precisely, the thought perhaps of his distance and unavailability to us, is at times an obstacle as we begin prayer. The sense of his withdrawal on some days can seem a hard, indisputable fact, a painful truth of prayer, turning us on ourselves in prayer when our most pressing need as we begin a time of silent prayer is to disappear from our own eyes. In those times, we have to refuse even a glance at ourselves. The soul afflicted by its own solitary state has no need of a mirror to examine its face. Even a brief look at ourselves may encourage erroneous conclusions. The most common mistake may be to arrive at a conviction of God's displeasure at our inadequacies and the abject failures he observes in us. Any attention directed to ourselves accentuates these distortions. If not checked, the exaggerations cause turbulence and upheaval. The actual truth of his abiding love in this particular hour will vanish. It is true that Our Lord might seem to us absent, detached, unyielding, but this is a false perspective of our own making. It is an entry into deception to think God has ever disappeared from us.

∼

Prayer in silence can seem on some days like the pursuit of a quick, beautiful animal darting ahead and disappearing, eluding our chase, ever beyond our glimpse. In a similar manner, God often seems reluctant to allow us even a moment's glance behind the veil of his mysterious presence. The effort each day can seem to confirm our incapacity to get any closer to him. Perhaps it helps to realize that the pursuit we undertake in prayer is less ours to direct than we think. In fact, seeking God in prayer may require us to drop all pretense of a pursuit. We cannot make a target of God in prayer, as though he were a prize that might be captured at some point. The elusive pursuit we resume each day does not permit illusions of this sort. In that sense, our difficulties in prayer ought not to be misinterpreted. God is never running from us, fleeing into the shadows that seem to surround us. Although he hides in concealment and mystery, it is not behind a barrier of absence. Rather, he waits in hiding; he waits for his hidden presence to be recognized in a manner we do not expect but, nonetheless, must learn to expect. After a while, it should not be unusual as we pray before the quiet of a tabernacle for a conviction of his hidden presence to flame up in our heart. Suddenly we know as clearly as sunlight that he is there in front of us, ever unseen before the incapacity of our eyes. And this sense of immediate presence may be entirely different from the day before in prayer, when he did not seem close at all. Perhaps only in such shifting experiences of certainty and inconclusiveness does he allow us contact with his mysterious presence. Let us be grateful for his gifts, even when they are sparing and infrequent. Whenever his actual nearness is embraced, his concealment vanishes, but of course not to our visible eye. The veil that covers our soul lifts for a moment, and he is with us. The chase is over temporarily, and we can rest for a time in the anchoring truth of his immediate presence. And for that, even if it is once in a lifetime, we must be forever grateful.

~

If the strain of trying to think about God seems to lead nowhere in our prayer, we have perhaps arrived at a propitious juncture in prayer. Our nothingness before God's infinite grandeur is a recognition easier to accept when our thought has been overcome in the silence of prayer. If that is to happen, we must not permit a painful frustration of mind to interpret our experience of prayer. The incapacity of our mind to lay hold of any insight in prayer can be a deceptive experience construed as a failure of prayer. If not understood properly, the mind's difficulties can lead to an exaggerated sense of our ineptitude in prayer. But there are better things in prayer than arriving at exalted thoughts. The blinding of our mind in prayer, the experience of being silenced in thought before a presence we cannot see, is often a more profound grace of prayer. The fact that we cannot take with us a tangible mental fruit from this experience in prayer does not signify a lesser form of prayer. For many people, the stifling of their minds and inability to move in prayer are the first serious graces pointing to a greater love for prayer. They are also the first noticeable sufferings in crossing the more serious thresholds of deeper contemplative prayer.

~

The frustration in prayer of God withdrawing again into darkness, eluding our search, just when he seemed near is by no means only an early test of silent prayer. Perhaps it never disappears from the life of prayer. Regrettably, many souls seem to experience God's return to concealment and shadows as a sign they are not meant for serious prayer and closeness to God. Others, on the other hand, come to know a longing for God that intensifies amid these frustrations. The question, nonetheless, remains how to conduct ourselves in a healthy manner before the daunting experience of God's penchant for hiding and so to avoid setbacks or mistakes in prayer. When God seems cut off from us, withholding himself, our desire for him may also seem blocked and inaccessible. We may suffer the incapacity to feel a desire for him, which can be a hard suffering. In that time, we must trust in the subdued presence of a desire for God at a deeper region of the soul that is not easy to confirm. We must trust that it awaits our discovery and will not be readily experienced, certainly not by means of emotion. Those who remain resolute in silent prayer, not giving up, are likely to encounter this deeper longing for God in their soul precisely because it does not leave them in peace and sooner or later manifests itself. It is known inasmuch as a need for prayer continues to demand attention. The hunger for prayer rises up at times, insisting on being heard. Yet giving oneself to quiet prayer for an extended time before a tabernacle seems to assuage it only temporarily. Afterward our soul may feel itself drawn once more to prayer, suffering if the opportunity is not present and we are left waiting. If we respond to this hunger, seeking even small chances to be with God alone in our soul, the beginning of a different awareness of God may soon be felt. Once the hunger is recognized with the reverence we might accord a special gift, a passion for God is likely never to depart from our life.

∼

"The more He wants to give, the more He makes us desire" (Saint John of the Cross, Letters, *Collected Works*). The inner distress that may linger after what seems nothing but empty, dry silence in prayer—receiving not even crumbs from the table —may actually be a good sign that a real encounter with God in prayer has taken place. There is great irony, naturally, in departing from prayer feeling weary, frustrated, more alone, precisely after God has touched the soul in some mysterious manner. Yet later in a day, we may discover the effects of this touch in an inflamed desire for God at deeper, unfelt regions of the soul. There is an important lesson of prayer here. The *experience* we undergo while praying may contradict the *truth* of prayer for the soul. But we do not realize this easily. The fire of a pure desire for God may burn at concealed depths, beneath our recognition. We have to trust that truth. As long as we want God alone, and nothing else, we have some assurance that a hidden flame of love is burning that we cannot see. On the other hand, those who expect this fire to make itself felt in heat and warmth will likely be disappointed. The rules of prayer contain no provisions for compensation or reward. We should not leave prayer like laborers stretching out our hands for payment at the end of a workday. God adopts his own manner of secret conduct and favor toward those he most loves. He takes measure of the purity of our desire for himself, and perhaps that alone. If he extends a sense of satisfaction at the end of silent prayer, it is typically to intensify a purer desire for himself and, often, to grant nothing more.

~

It takes much faith to accept that a desire for God while suffering dry, desolate emptiness in prayer can be a purer expression of attachment to God than a fiery love fed by emotion. Of course, this may not seem so to our soul. But we are helped if we ponder the depth of purification that God apparently seeks in souls dear to him. It may surprise us that the most courageous souls concealed in cloisters and monasteries suffer at times wondering whether the chronic weariness felt in their prayer is a sign perhaps that they are wasting their lives. The distance from God that their emptiness of feeling seems to indicate can be a nettling goad, often impossible to overcome. In that sense, the purification of faith these souls undergo has rarely to do with any doubt of doctrinal truth. It has much to do, rather, with doubts about their own worthiness, a loss of conviction that their own soul has any attraction for God. The suffering can be great when a life given fully to God finds itself after some years in a dusty corner of inescapable, interior isolation. Yet these courageous souls continue to desire and long for God, persevering in love, even as they seem to possess no internal evidence of love. The absence of felt closeness to God may at times deceive them, but it does not undermine them. They are often heroic in love through such times, finding ways to offer to God from a poor beggar's purse. Over time the sacrificial subtleties of their lives may assume a great appeal before the eyes of God. There is nothing meager in their pure desire to give; their generosities can be intense in the small ways of great love. They may feel nothing in their inner spirit but empty weariness, yet they continue to give. Without their knowledge, they are perhaps the treasures and jewels of the divine desire to see a soul pruned down to its nothingness out of great love for him.

~

Aridity in prayer may be God's work of purification, but it requires a cooperation and an interior mental austerity, remembering that in time it bears fruit. The emptying of emotion from our prayer allows us to know better our true nothingness before the immensity of God. In dryness we become more insignificant in our own eyes, more humbled and prostrate toward God. Aridity in prayer must be left to run its course, not as a form of illness that must be healed or as a reason for complaint or disappointment with God. The truth is that it casts our soul more nakedly before the concealment of the divine presence. God remains always a mystery of transcendent otherness even in his intimacy with souls. His mystery of unfathomed love is the premise for every possibility of contact with him. In a certain paradoxical manner, feeling nothing in prayer becomes itself a taste of God's transcendent mystery. Perhaps only in the abasement of a tangibly felt nothingness can our intimacy with the true mystery of God deepen. As the soul grows in contemplative graces, greater union with God depends in part on the transcendence of God overwhelming our awareness of our poverty. Yet, at other times, usually less commonly, prayer can be effortless in its receptivity to God when an intense desire for God is felt within the soul. A pure longing seems to come from some depth within our soul, which turns blindly in the direction of an unseen personal presence. And where might he be hiding, the person of Our Lord? Can a location be sought? The soul does not need to search for a place or location. The sooner it realizes this truth, the more stable is prayer, despite any sense of dry, naked emptiness. It is enough to know only that the tides of desire drawing us from some concealed depth within our soul confirm his presence. He hides somewhere in the stillness underneath our soul's longing.

~

Courage in prayer requires a perseverance in difficult interior states without apparent remedy, with no way at times out of a thick weariness and fatigue of soul. The martyrs have perhaps something to teach us regarding this contemplative endurance in prayer. In some cases, the courage of Christian martyrs in facing death reached its climatic point, not in torture, but before the ordeal of pain commenced, when it became evident that no rescue would take place. When they realized there would be no escape and they would soon die, in many cases they must have made a great offering of their lives to God. Prior to any actual physical pain, they let go and offered. This could not be done without a pure love for God. The example may be somewhat similar when a soul in prayer suffers an inner desolation that does not disappear for a long period of time. A pure desire to love God when the spirit feels crushed and can find no relief requires a response like a martyr's surrender to death. In a naked poverty stripped of options, we must reject illusion, refusing the thought of some imminent rescue. It is a poverty, moreover, in which the desire to offer to God a gift of ourselves must entertain no fantasy of heroism. The nothingness of our soul cannot become a personal drama, as though this condition of inner desolation somehow exalted us. The simple truth is always far better. If our soul has entered a desert of naked inner darkness, and God seems to be far away beyond a distant horizon, this is precisely the hour of surrender for a soul. The emptiness is a propitious condition for a pure act of love to pierce hidden depths within the soul.

~

In professing our unworthiness in prayer, we admit a truth before God. But we do not speak the whole truth by that acknowledgment. We are unworthy, we are inept, we are incapable, but these are still just half-truths. Under God's mysterious gaze and in the presence of his silent, unfathomable word spoken to the depth of our soul, we are known and loved. Our unworthiness before God does not obstruct his vision and his loving gaze cast upon the depths of our soul. In a way we cannot conceive, God may love us much more in the hour when confused thoughts churn in our mind or frustrations pervade our intellect than in an hour when all seems bright and clear. We do not know what God perceives in the deeper vulnerabilities of our soul, and we can never know. If we seek him with a pure desire, what we seem not to understand or grasp may signify very little. What is known to God is the desire of the soul at its purest level of concentration, and that truth is quite hidden ordinarily from our own view.

∽

Early on in a life of prayer, the thought of our nothingness without God ought to be firmly embraced, precisely because it does not draw on easy recognition. Before long, though, if we are serious in prayer, it is not difficult to return our thought to our nothingness and absolute need for God. It even becomes our comfort in prayer on some days. At that point in time, we really do not need to cultivate the thought of our nothingness. We need only to hide ourselves within this truth of our nothingness and allow it to carry us closer to the heart of Our Lord. Once we are sufficiently aware that we are nothing without him, we need not dwell anxiously on this truth, as though probing it might reveal a more comfortable truth. The stark realization in itself of our nothingness apart from him seems to draw his presence closer to us, as though this conviction were somehow a key that opens a door with God. And from then on it is not surprising that God manifests this truth more often in humiliations, in small failures, in our foolish mistakes, making us ever more convinced that we are in truth nothing at all without him.

5

Simplicity toward the Common Quandaries

In this nakedness the spirit finds its quietude and rest. For in coveting nothing, nothing raises it up and nothing weighs it down, because it is in the center of its humility. When it covets something in this very desire it is wearied.

—Saint John of the Cross,
The Ascent of Mount Carmel

Prayer consists of attention. It is the orientation of all the attention of which the soul is capable towards God. The quality of the attention counts for much in the quality of the prayer. Warmth of heart cannot make up for it.

—Simone Weil,
Waiting for God

I always find very fulfilling that way of looking for Our Lord in what he is not . . . each time I feel him hidden even more, concealed more, incomprehensible even more.

—Saint Maria Maravillas of Jesus
(unpublished quotation, Brooklyn Carmel)

The daily effort of prayer might seem to call for skills and a proficiency in method. But the mysterious realm of prayer does not respond well to a notion of advancement by native or developed ability. This is a graced enterprise of deepening personal relations with God himself, not of acquired skills. Every soul of serious prayer must confront its own incapacities in prayer. The mind, in particular, can be an uncooperative faculty in prayer. At the same time, there are deeper truths of personal engagement with God meant to take place in prayer even as we undergo the trials of our inadequacy to pray well. We learn over time that love is the one thing needful in prayer, indeed, on some days the only thing possible. What our mind is or is not capable of plays a secondary role to the essential purpose of prayer, which is to draw our soul into a deeper love for God and his will. "The important thing is not to think much but to love much; and so do that which best stirs you to love" (Saint Teresa of Avila, The Interior Castle).

Perhaps technique and method are useless in prayer after a while, if a soul has been generous in love. A deeper love does not respond so well to methods and finds them a distraction, even scoffing at them. Once a threshold of love in prayer has been crossed, directions and instructions seem only to interfere. Exercises to undertake, steps and programs to follow, draw resistance almost as an offense against love. Rather, something veiled and hidden, something never explained or fully understood, now attracts in prayer. No self-conscious effort, no seeking to measure or acquire, no concern for progress is permitted. A gaze of the soul on its own experience will not gain access to the deeper secret of the Beloved's near presence. The soul comes to know that Our Lord draws closer only when it is not watching, not waiting for a confirmation of his presence. Technique and method can serve no purpose for this; they are relics of the past. Now the Beloved Lord alone determines the rhythm of mutual love in prayer. The length of his delay in returning and the duration of his favor when he comes are solely his choice. The soul that loves learns to surrender to him in simplicity and without expectation. And for that there is no method or technique in prayer, only the effort of love itself and a willingness to humble oneself.

∽

The imaginative visualization of a scene from the Gospel can certainly be a way of focusing prayer. But too strict a discipline in any method of meditation may place restrictions on prayer that Our

Lord might prefer us to relax a bit. We sometimes forget that the goal of prayer is primarily to deepen our relations of love with God, and this implies a certain unpredictability in the time of prayer. What we start out "looking at" in prayer is sometimes quickly blanketed in shadow despite our efforts and quickly disappears from sight. Likewise, the words of Scripture that initially hold our mind with some interest may abruptly collapse into fragments and fade away as if the wind had suddenly caught and scattered them. What seems at first a failure of this sort may actually conceal an invitation to relinquish our sense of control over prayer and allow the hand of another to take over, namely, God's hand. We have to accept that sometimes he prefers to turn off the lights and leave us like a person lost and unable to see, stumbling in the direction of an unseen voice faintly heard in the distance. Indeed, we learn in time that what God seems most to desire are encounters with himself that will be poor and unsupported by any ability on our part.

~

When Mother Teresa was still alive and on a visit outside India, if the option had been offered to a group of her sisters for one sister to volunteer to be her traveling companion on a long plane trip *or* instead to gather that same evening with the sisters in the convent after the plane's departure and watch a new, award-winning documentary of Mother Teresa, it is safe to say that no one in her congregation of the Missionaries of Charity would have preferred to watch the film. The desire to travel at Mother Teresa's side on that plane would have been a universal choice. Even if she needed to sleep the entire journey, none of her sisters would have wanted to miss this chance. Watching a beloved person on a film screen could not compare to being in the close presence of that person, even if she was sleeping soundly in the next seat on a plane. Perhaps we need to remember that difference when in our prayerful meditations on the Gospel we are frustrated at our failure to think insightful thoughts or enjoy vivid images, while all along in that hour we have before us, indescribably close, the silent presence of Our Lord in a tabernacle.

~

God showing himself to our soul is never for dramatic effect. He does not intend by the graces of prayer to award us with some form of a spiritual trophy that can be placed on a private mantlepiece for admiration. When God does show himself, he takes great care always to preserve his hiddenness. It would seem he prefers not to shed more than thin layers of disguise. His mystery remains intact and only partially disclosed. The result is contrary to every naive expectation of a comforting experience of God in prayer. He is more likely to make us ache with continual desire for him than to satisfy at some point a longing for intimacy with him. Indeed, the drama of prayer ordinarily plays out in a setting of dim shadows and indefinite encounters. The place of encounter for our deeper relations with God is a subdued bare corner of the soul. We often know only later, after the conclusion of prayer, the gift of his immediate presence in the hour just completed. In the darkened enclosure of prayer, we learn to exercise faith more intensely, more blindly, with more dependence on love. It is precisely this experience of deeper faith that brings the certainty of his actual unfathomable favor to our soul.

∼

What we cannot grasp in our thought of God in prayer and cannot perceive, we should not attempt to *experience*. The inclination to grope toward some manner of experiencing God may be a reaction to a dissatisfaction in not being able to arrive at some clear thought of God. When we do not face properly the deeper mystery of God and do not accept quietly his ultimate incomprehensibility, perhaps we seek some form of an immediate experience go on day after day. Yet the effect on prayer of this frustration may be surprisingly fruitful. At the least, it intensifies a longing for God that can become a consuming passion in our soul. A great and even immense desire for giving ourselves entirely to God is often the consequence of many days of casting our line in prayer and catching no fish.

~

A steady discipline of mind is required in the effort of prayer. Initially, we are attempting to place ourselves before the presence of the invisible God of mystery. The mental discipline is in part to accept the parameters of prayer, what is possible and what is not. A direct experience of Our Lord does not occur in prayer, if by that we mean a direct, immediate experience enjoyed by our senses. The experience of prayer takes place, rather, in the interior realm of receptivity to God. Prayer is a receptive surrender to him in faith and love, dependent most of all on our interior offering to him. It is true that our senses may enjoy the quiet setting of a chapel conducive to peaceful prayer, but Our Lord speaks in prayer, not primarily to our senses, but rather to our inner soul. It may be easy in a peaceful state of prayer to imagine him talking to us, but the thought risks illusion. The essential task is rather to live prayer in faith and bear his actual silence. Deeper prayer consists, not so much in an exchange of words, but in the silent communication of eyes gazing at each other. Unfortunately, our own eyes are blind and see nothing, while his eyes pierce the inner depths of our soul with love. The act of prayer must acknowledge that penetrating look of Our Lord cast upon the center of our soul. We are known to him, and this recognition is more than enough for any hour of prayer. The awareness of his gaze on our soul can always draw us to the offering of a renewed surrender to him.

∼

The temptation to drift in prayer almost mindlessly toward an abstract, impersonal notion of God may need to be conquered at times by learning to call upon Our Lord's name in a fresh manner as though for the first time. But this means we must speak his name with a great loving reverence, with a conviction of his near presence, and from an intense desire for his close friendship. This is no magical act of incantation but, rather, a trust in the actual words of Jesus at the Last Supper. "If you ask anything in my name, I will do it" (Jn 14:14). Often the first request we need to make in prayer is precisely the recovery of his presence in the quiet of our heart, even if it is true that he has never departed. The slow repetition of his name in the Jesus prayer—

"Lord Jesus Christ, Son of God, have mercy on me, a sinner"—is a way to recover a deep conviction of his presence within us. We can do this almost in the same manner that we meet someone in his home when we cross a threshold into a room where that person awaits us. Prayer is contact and encounter with a real person, with our feet firmly planted on the ground, our eyes turned in the direction of a face, even if unseen. No one meets another person in an enclosed room by staring abstractly at the ceiling or looking out the window. We gaze directly in the direction of a face and a voice. We must remember that the same thing is required in prayer.

～

"Nothing is more essential to prayer than attentiveness" (Evagrius Ponticus, *The Praktikos and Chapters on Prayer*). Distancing ourselves from God in prayer is at times excused as a difficulty with distracting thoughts. But these thoughts that take us from God may be an attractive alternative to prayer more than we admit and not so unwelcome as we claim. The common sight today of people with cell phones reading text messages while sitting in a pew in a church is a modern image of the perennial struggle to give to God all our attention in prayer. Prayerful concentration is possible only when we are deeply aware in faith of his actual presence close to us, even within our heart and soul. In the current hour in any Catholic Church, we kneel or stand or sit directly before God himself in Our Lord's Eucharistic presence in a tabernacle. The thought of his presence, and his actual humanity in front of us, are an antidote to every casual approach to prayer. Distraction and restlessness in prayer seem to dissipate quickly when we linger in a loving gaze on the tabernacle in front of our eyes, where Our Lord hides from us and yet watches us from his hiding place. This realization of being in the presence of God himself in the Blessed Sacrament always fosters a respect for the sacredness of prayer.

∽

Every vague, unaccountable restlessness in our spirit can make it difficult initially to settle down in a time of silent prayer. How can we turn our thoughts properly to God when we cannot turn our agitated attention away from our own affairs? The restlessness can exercise at times a resilient hold on consciousness, and there may be no good cause to explain it. Our soul then seems simply trapped in the drifting movement of its own wandering, with no escape from the waves of scattering thought that interfere with prayer. Perhaps all we can do then is to offer our lack of freedom to a merciful God, knowing that all things are passing, including the current condition of what seems a very poor prayer. God blesses our soul for the desire we have to be with him. Whether we are successful or not in our own estimation of prayer matters perhaps very little.

~

"Prayer is thinking of him while loving him" (Blessed Charles de Foucauld, *The Spiritual Autobiography*). The fragmentation of our interior life into disparate thoughts and desires that dance haphazardly in and out of awareness during a silent time of prayer can make a wholehearted love for God seem a near impossible venture. The apparent indiscipline of mind and heart can become almost a reproach to our soul, especially when so many trivial, disconnected matters press for notice. The unsettled interior state and the inability to overcome it can seem almost emblematic of our unsuitability for a deeper pursuit of God. And yet just when discouragement is most sharp and biting in this regard, a humble acknowledgment of our inadequacy in prayer may please God much more than a renewed exertion of effort. Prayer, we must not forget, is a relationship with someone for a lifetime, for better or for worse. After a certain point, there is no need to secure God's favor in our life of prayer. At best we are poor souls, and yet accepted and much loved by him all the same.

∿

In every healthy conviction of faith, there is a combination of tendencies—an inclination to conserve what is treasured in knowledge as well as a demand for new discovery. It may be that new insights and discoveries surprise us in prayer precisely when we reflect on truths of faith that we already know. These truths contain wellsprings of mystery that are never tapped sufficiently. The turn to familiar truths in prayer may begin uneventfully but may end in a thought never before considered. Grace is of course behind this phenomenon. But we should realize also that the new thought we have received may be part of a series of insights we can anticipate as forthcoming in the succeeding days of prayer. These thoughts may often come from our attention to the words of Jesus in the Gospel. When words in a Gospel passage suddenly resonate with a sense of immediate encounter with Our Lord, it is time to pause in the sacredness of that moment. The two Emmaus disciples asked Our Lord to "stay with us" (Lk 24:29), and he immediately responded to their appeal. Perhaps he cannot resist those three words from any of us. The deep conviction that he will remain for a time with us after we make this appeal, before vanishing again, is a truth that can be recovered in prayer repeatedly. Indeed, all our most profound experiences of God in prayer echo this request for him to "stay with me" for even a short time.

~

When in the first chapter of the Gospel of Saint John, Jesus says that he saw Nathaniel under the fig tree, and Nathaniel immediately exclaims, "Rabbi, you are the Son of God! You are the King of Israel!" (Jn 1:49), it is an example of a cryptic moment in the Gospel that hides a further possibility. What was Nathaniel doing as he stood under the shade of that fig tree? We should not imagine that he was looking for figs. Was he, rather, in an intense moment of prayer, pondering the current circumstances, as many of us do at times, in his case beseeching God that he might be blessed to see the presence of the Messiah during his lifetime? We know in fact that there was a strong expectation among religious people of the time that the coming of the Messiah was likely and imminent. A prayer of that sort is entirely plausible. Nathaniel apparently received Jesus' observation of seeing him under the fig tree, not as a casual remark, but as a significant revelation in itself. And why so? Nathaniel perhaps was bent down and hiding his face in prayer while

standing behind that tree. Jesus' statement that he
saw him there, saw him as he prayed in a private fer-
vor of longing to see the Messiah one day, is what
may have struck Nathaniel so forcibly. For only
God himself can see us in our concealed prayer;
only he hears the silent words we speak in the secrecy of our heart; only he can answer a prayer so
quickly. It is he alone who can favor us, as he did
with Nathaniel, with an immediate, overwhelming
reply when we long with desire for him.

～

"Enter by the narrow gate" (Mt 7:13). An example of a small remark of Jesus, but one that can
echo poignantly when we hear the questions that
may accompany it—"Do you want this? Will you
do this for me? Can you offer me this gift?" The
Gospel invites us to hear these questions echoing in
the silence after we read many statements of Jesus
from the Gospel. Each of the beatitudes, for instance, is enhanced by hearing them. These questions challenge our soul to recognize the importance of a choice. They can provoke us to hear an
invitation that we have not yet considered. These
questions can incite a quest for a more personal
approach to love that we must now pursue more
intently. Often, they cannot be answered without
some form of waiting and attentiveness, lingering

on the words of Jesus. Before an answer is offered, some inner depth of soul must be penetrated with longing, and for this we must wait. The presence of this longing in our soul is a sign that the desire to give more to Our Lord is stirring within our soul. For some time, it can seem that any question of this sort keeps returning to a concealed place within the soul, waiting for the day it will be heard clearly. And that day will demand a choice and a concrete response. We will find we have to repeat an answer throughout life, "yes, Lord, I want all that you ask, all that will please you."

∼

When we do answer, the response is of course not by words alone or simply by a thought. Words can give a correct reply, thoughts can be filled with clarity and insight. But these questions of our desire to be one with God's desire are directed to the heart much more than simply the mind. For that reason, the answer we offer is never complete, never conclusive, only a step toward some commitment in decisive action. By their nature, questions of this sort can be given no definitive answer that puts that demand for action to rest. The questions seem always to return again, often in a slightly altered guise. They sometimes return swiftly, other times after long delay, even years. In some cases, when

the return of a question from Our Lord comes unexpectedly, the inner spirit finds itself caught off-
guard, shaken, and can offer no clear reply. The
incapacity to answer touches something deeper in
the soul. It may be the reason why these questions
from God occur with no notice or prior hint. They
are meant to carry us to the mystery of the presence of God speaking within them.

～

Sometimes it may happen that we forget to ask God
what we were going to request in prayer because
our prayer that day became forgetful of self and
we did not remember to make our request. Yet
this neglect does not seem to impede God from
hearing our petition in any case. Sometimes he
seems to respond more favorably in such instances
when we have not made an explicit request. Perhaps he is pleased by the forgetfulness of self and
delights in the purer selflessness. At times we may
only remember what we forgot to ask when we
later receive the favor we never requested. When
we are inattentive to ourselves during prayer because our longing for God is intense, it seems that
he often listens to our unspoken desire, without
a need for a description in exact words. We can
assume Our Lord loves the soul oblivious to itself
because in that hour its desire is consumed with

him. He treats the soul then like a young child who cannot be faulted for losing a train of thought when that child wants really only to cling to the hand of his father or mother.

$\sim$

"Let us return to the heart, that we may find Him" (Saint Augustine in Ratzinger, *Behold the Pierced One*). An act of pure desire for God's will, if we can embrace it fully, is what a saint's love may have been in a continuous manner. If so, we should try never to leave silent prayer without striving to make such an act. Perhaps we have only to choose a pure desire for God's will even once, and its impact will make itself known rather quickly. It may carve an intense need within our soul unmatched by any other effort in prayer. Indeed, an interior attraction for such an act may quickly be felt. The pure desire for God's will can be like a release of our heart in prayer for which we have long waited. It is never finished but demands ever purer acts of greater intensity. We may find that a deep inner need summons us to repeat these acts as a primary sustenance in every silent hour of prayer. They will answer a longing for God in our soul beyond any other comfort we can seek in prayer.

6

The Holy Mystery of Transcendence

What strikes the mind so forcibly and so painfully is His absence (if I may so speak) from His own world. It is a silence that speaks. It is as if others had got possession of His work. Why does not He, our Maker and Ruler, give us some immediate knowledge of Himself?

—Saint John Henry Newman,
Grammar of Assent

God is not merely the infinite abyss or the infinite apex, sustaining everything, but never entering finitude. God is not merely infinite distance, but also infinite proximity. One can entrust oneself to him: He listens and sees and loves.

—Joseph Ratzinger (Gaál,
The Theology of Pope Benedict XVI)

If God conceals himself, it is in his very presence. His transcendence does not mean that he is exiled from the world; it is the exact opposite of an absence.

—Henri de Lubac, S.J.,
The Discovery of God

Respect for the magnitude of utter mystery in God can be at times in tension with a deeply felt desire in prayer to experience God in a personal manner. Prayer as it advances contemplatively is animated by a deep longing to love and be united to God. But always there must be a realization that God cannot be held down and confined within our private experience of prayer. A harmony of truths must balance in prayer, including metaphysical truths. God is a transcendent mystery to be adored and loved; he is equally our Beloved Lord who becomes one with our own body in the reception of the Eucharist. His being is beyond our comprehension and grasp, yet he is known in adoration and admiring awe. Contemplative love is perhaps most fully itself in blind prostration before the incomprehensible mystery of God. An engagement with divine transcendence is an aspect of deeper faith and love that will always accompany deeper contemplative life. "Surely we have the right not to see God? . . . And in not knowing him, I recognise him" (Paul Claudel, in Henri de Lubac, The Discovery of God).

All seeking of God in silent prayer entails a form of spiritual experience. Yet the possibilities for experiences in prayer offer a wide spectrum and variation, not all equal in value, not all healthy. Seeking God in prayer depends on the steady exercise of a sober and patient faith; imagination and emotional impression are secondary elements and sometimes deceptive. Since the latter enter into the experience of prayer, it is good to be clear about what is ordinarily possible to experience in our relations with the divine. The transcendent mystery of a hidden God is an essential truth. It ought not to be forgotten or neglected or remain far from our thought. Without a clear sense that God is transcendent and hidden in his immutable mystery and beyond our immediate human grasp, we risk false notions in the claim of a direct experience of God. Yet this hazard seems to occur frequently. The desire for direct experiences of God, and the claim of receiving them, is not unusual. The assertion of private messages from God is likewise common today, at least in certain circles. The conviction of God speaking words of enlightenment or instruction presumes an accessibility to God that is improbable. In all likelihood, a confusion is taking place due to an overheated imagination. For some people, it is imperative for truth's sake to tame desires for intoxicated "experiences" of God and simply to accept the ordinary path of sober faith. A deep contemplative relationship with God in faith can be both profound and yet empty of extraordinary experiences. And that is apparently what God usually wills and chooses for souls of serious prayer. We forget perhaps too easily that the primary path to God is always by way of generous, sacrificial affinity for his will, in whatever way this is shown and demanded in our lives.

~

The current era in the Church continues to be a
time of confusion in spirituality and of unexamined
notions about prayer. For some decades now, a lack
of sobriety and rootedness in Catholic spiritual tra-
ditions has encouraged experimentation in spirituality. Eclectic approaches have flourished, mixing
incongruous and discordant elements into the life
of prayer. A desire for interior "experiences" has
fueled a false notion that methods of prayer can offer pathways into the esoteric realm of personal encounters with God. Sometimes this has meant the
uncritical adoption of Buddhist or Hindu forms
of prayer as a way of enhancing the experience of
Christian prayer. What is not considered perhaps
is that the doctrine of God in non-Christian reli-
gions will affect the approach to prayer itself. If
a religion professes that God is unknown in any
personal sense, as Buddhism affirms, the prayer itself will not seek to encounter a personal God.
If a religion professes multiple gods, as Hinduism
does, it is difficult to see why Jesus Christ is anything more than a special avatar among a collection
of deities. Prayer and belief always have a correla-
tion. And Christian prayer has an essential foundation in a proper doctrinal understanding of God
—a transcendent God who has revealed himself in
Jesus Christ. It is impossible to embrace ideas about

God in prayer that conflict with Catholic doctrine and not suffer ill effects.

～

"The root of false mysticism is the yearning to 'have experiences'" (Thomas Merton, foreword to William Johnston, *The Mysticism of the Cloud of Unknowing*). The presumption that an experiential encounter with God is available for pursuit through prayer techniques, and that he makes himself accessible through these methods to the direct experience of souls, is often accepted without question. But this idea is contrary to the sound tradition of Christian spirituality. The Catholic tradition of prayer presupposes a serious effort of virtue as a necessary foundation for prayer. When, by contrast, direct experiences of the divine are sought as an end in themselves, the pursuit of prayer is often unaccompanied by any need for interior purification and sacrifice for the sake of union with the will of God. The dominant focus is rather on the cultivation of an interior ambiance of inner silence and peacefulness. When this is duly achieved, usually by means of mind-emptying meditation methods, the claim is often made that a bodily experience of meditative tranquility is a clear sign and indication of experiencing God. The senses purportedly confirm by their enjoyment of peace the immediate

proximity of God to the soul. But this claim of
direct, tangible experiences of God by means of
meditation methods contradicts the testimony of
traditional Catholic spirituality, which affirms that
if God is truly encountered, this takes place ordinarily in a depth of silence within the soul, in
transcendent mystery and in a certain ineffability.
The interior stillness of soul in the reception of
genuine contemplative graces does not cease to remain a place of concealment for the transcendent
presence of God.

~

In a somewhat similar way, it is possible that emotional impressionability fuels the confidence in God's
direct instructions guiding in the lives of those
who make a strong claim for the charismatic authority of the Holy Spirit in their lives. The opportunity for error is subtle and beguiling. People
convinced of being favored by God do not easily subject their conviction to a critical examina-
tion. They tend to resist any form of outside questioning; the reluctance is understandable. In many
cases, an attachment to the inner satisfaction of receiving special communications from God is a non-
negotiable perception. The charismatic experience
of God has melded over time with faith itself in
a very personal manner. The thought of relations

with God without special experiences may have become unthinkable. But this may simply indicate that a dependency on an experiential confirmation of God's love enjoyed by the emotions and senses has been for too long an inflexible and dominating perception of relations with God. Absent is a deeper awareness of the contemplative need to receive God in silence and emptiness. The words of Saint John of the Cross that God is properly sought as one who is perpetually hidden, indeed incomprehensible and inaccessible to the immediate experience of the senses and emotions, would seem to be of importance in such cases.

$\sim$

The question can be asked by anyone serious about prayer: Is an experience of the transcendent possible? Or does this term designate a realm of reality that precludes any direct experience? Is a transcendent, hidden God by definition beyond all possible encounter and experience? These questions would seem pertinent for every soul open to contemplative graces. Let it be said first that the meaning of the word transcendent in a Christian context must have reference to the Incarnation of Jesus Christ. If God has spoken to us in a distinct manner in his eternal Word, his Son, Jesus Christ, then an immediate encounter with divine truth is possible.

An experience of the transcendent God can take place any time we rest silently in the presence of the words of Jesus speaking from the Gospel. Even more, we find ourselves face to face with the sublimity of transcendent truth any time we kneel before a tabernacle. In the presence of the Eucharist, the mystery of God himself is immediately accessible before our blind eyes. By faith we can have an experience of his hidden presence even as it is incomprehensible to any purely rational effort of explanation. The profound encounter with God's loving presence in praying before a tabernacle or monstrance never removes the reality of his utter mystery. His transcendent truth as the God of otherness and mystery remains always concealed on the far side of a barrier we cannot cross on our own in this life. Indeed, this infinite transcendence of God is precisely what we do experience at times in a prayer of deeper encounter with him. The transcendent mystery of God is known in prayer, not so much intellectually, not because we choose to think about it, but as a truth cutting to the core of our being, overcoming our mind. In fact, even more so, it cuts into our heart sharply on any day that we love him with an awareness of his infinite grandeur.

∿

The conviction of God's presence in the silence of prayer is a private experience for a soul. Yet to speak of it as private does not suggest a subjective notion that has no evident confirmation. When a soul is receptive in faith in praying before a tabernacle, God's presence in prayer is unquestionably real for that soul. The conviction is often inseparable from a desire the soul then has to give itself to God. Without the soul's desire to give itself in return, the presence of God in prayer likely makes less impact and might even be questioned. This sense of God's real presence that accompanies a more intense desire for him has nothing to do with a mood or feeling in the hour of prayer. It is a certitude of faith that deepens progressively over time. The fact that it is an experience unique and private to a particular soul does not cast doubt on its reality. The private experience in prayer is never simply private, never something we engage in alone. For God is the beloved companion of every soul in the experience of prayer. The experience in prayer on any day remains a singular and mysterious contact with God. But at the same time, it is an experience that has a real cause and undeniable reality behind it, namely, Our Lord himself. If we are praying before a tabernacle, this truth is evident. The hidden, transcendent God steps out of hiding in some manner and makes himself known to the soul who loves him and longs for him. The soul of deeper prayer has no need to examine the matter. What happens in prayer while in the presence of God is simply all too real.

~

The presence of Jesus in the Gospel standing before crowds or alone in front of a Peter or a Mary Magdalen entailed a direct encounter with God. These face-to-face encounters with Jesus contained in themselves the heart of all mystery, even as they remained human encounters. Always it was the case that the presence of Jesus as a man was hiding a transcendent truth of divine mystery that was never sufficiently grasped. Even Mary his mother might say that she embraced the truth of his divine presence by a progressive entry into the transcendent mystery of divine concealment. For Mary, the reality of Our Lord's divine presence unveiled its truth from his conception onward within mundane, everyday occurrences. The touch of Jesus upon the hand of his mother, for instance, was for her an encounter with the touch of God himself in a direct and personal manner. Receiving his most ordinary words and observing his gestures were experiences in one sense beyond full comprehension because God himself was present in them. Likewise, for us, the words and the actions of Jesus can be understood, and yet these human words and actions conceal a hidden depth of divine presence that is beyond our complete possession. Indeed, the Gospel account hides a quality of truth continually beyond our understanding. And perhaps this is primarily what it means to be in the presence of the transcendent. The transcendent exceeds our capacity for a full comprehension, and yet this does not exclude the possibility of direct contact. The encounter is with transcendent mystery, and the presence of his mystery always draws the soul in love. This truth must animate our prayer. Perhaps with Mary's help, inasmuch as she lived in this manner herself, we can become in our silent prayer more childlike in our conviction of God in his divine presence sheltering us—like a small child content to remain at the father's side, safe beneath the shade and protection of a strong father holding that child's hand.

~

The importance of engaging God's transcendent mystery in faith can be appreciated by realizing what occurs when we lose this sense. But what is meant by the loss of a religious sense of transcendence? What does it signify for the life of faith? As a term of reference, the transcendent implies the existence of spiritual realities beyond our immediate and ordinary grasp. The reality of an invisible

God, for instance, transcends our ordinary capacity for perception. His concealed presence does not manifest itself openly to our human eyes. We know, of course, that our inability to see him does not mean that he is unreal. Rather, a veil of blindness covers our eyes, a barrier obstructs our perception, because the profound reality of God surpasses everything known of this world. Yet innumerable testimonies affirm that God can be known, he can be experienced. For souls of serious prayer, his presence as personal mystery is impossible to deny when he provokes within the soul sharp spiritual hungers to know him. A deep certitude of his presence always accompanies a deeper faith, and it is unshakeable. But what happens when the human capacity to turn with an open spirit in the direction of transcendent truth is blocked and we are unable to lift its eyes upward, as though something in our spirit were damaged and broken? Loss of the sense of transcendence will always cripple spiritual vision. What cannot be seen as a truth by the ordinary capacity of the eye is then not so much deliberately rejected as, rather, now ignored as if it did not exist. It draws no curiosity or interest. It is nonexistent inasmuch as it is not a part of the visible world. The loss of transcendent vision buries the soul in a limited, narrow perspective of the world. It can be like a confinement within prison walls, reduced to nearsightedness. We need always to protect our deeper sense of God's concealed proximity to our lives. For he is near us precisely in the hidden manner of his divine intimacy.

~

Loss of a sense of transcendence does not mean that religious faith dies as a consequence. Faith may continue to smolder at a low flame. Rather, what disappears in losing the sense of transcendence is an essential perception required for deeper spirituality and prayer. Without a sense of religious transcendence in the soul, an indifference or neglect toward the existence of invisible realities takes hold. In that regard, the loss of transcendence has immediate consequences. Respect for religious sacredness vanishes, reverence for the holy disappears. A receptive capacity to perceive them collapses. Even with the loss of transcendence, we may retain a certain allegiance to religious faith. But this often results in an externalized, bloodless faith when the holy is no longer recognized, when sacredness does not habitually prostrate a soul before God. Without a habit of transcendent perception, the unseen reality of divine presence evaporates and is no longer present before our eyes. The inclination to adore the truth of divine presence in our midst is no longer felt. The proximity of God as a personal presence may be replaced instead by mildly superstitious musings. Most tellingly, the Eucharist is no longer an attraction to the soul. The great transcendent gift of a deeper spiritual life to seek Our Lord in his near presence in a tabernacle drifts away and fades from a life.

～

"Somehow such things are known by a not know-ing, and so by this kind of knowing their mysteri-ousness is realized" (Saint Augustine, *City of God*, in Henry Chadwick, *Augustine*). The transcendence of the divine nature, completely other than our hu-man nature, is a truth that should be recovered pe-riodically within our prayer. The truth of God in his infinite mystery is indeed beyond our grasp and comprehension. But unless this same truth pro-vokes in us a need to discover the hidden presence of someone presently at home within our soul, gaz-ing upon our soul, the truth of God's transcendence can be transposed into an erroneous idea of our incapacity for deeply personal relations with God. An exclusive or fixated notion of God's transcen-dence without an awareness of Christ's face reveal-ing God to us can make relations with him seem impossible. He is in fact looking at us whenever we pray before him in the Blessed Sacrament. In praying before a tabernacle, we are not Muslims turning to an almighty God of unknown mystery and doing prostrations before a bare wall. The hidden presence of Our Lord in the Eucharist has a very different effect, and we must count this effect a supreme gift in our lives. The transcendent mystery of God intensifies as we pray before his concealed presence in the Eucharist. Yet at the same time, praying before him in the Eucharist reduces the sense of distance from God. The infinite mystery of God is encountered as an immediate personal presence in the silence of a nearby tabernacle. Our God has a voice and a face, even in silence and despite our visual blindness. As our incarnate Lord, he is a man offering us his divine presence. In the sacred Host, he is the incomprehensible fullness of God's humble beauty and attraction.

∼

Sometimes the doctrine of the divine indwelling in the soul is conceived to be a kind of "place" of interior enclosure in the soul that one needs only to "enter" for a direct experience of God to take place. But the indwelling of God within the soul does not remove the transcendent truth of God as One who is incomprehensible and inaccessible even as he dwells within us in grace. As Saint John of the Cross affirms forcefully, God's concealment remains a perpetual reality and intensifies even as he invites us to the intimacy of a companionship with himself. The last word on God's presence within the soul is always his infinite transcendence as our God of love. Any mild or stronger sense our soul might seem to enjoy of his presence within our soul is not to be interpreted as a "location" we have discovered and might easily return to. The place for encounter with him is the limitless truth of his presence in mystery. Divine love is not waiting for our soul to take hold of it as a possession within our soul that we can now claim belongs to us. Rather, Our Lord waits for our soul to surrender repeatedly to his love, which in itself conveys to us always a deeper sense of his transcendent and sacred mystery. It is surrender of soul that takes us to the divine encounter.

~

Until we begin to spend more time in silent prayer, we may not realize the need in prayer to seek a *transcendence* of ourselves. And yet this need to let go and extend beyond ourselves is precisely what Jesus commands in teaching us to lose ourselves for love of him. The invitation is not just in action but is at the very core of our being and, therefore, in the manner in which we turn to God in prayer. Self-transcendence in prayer means to pass beyond self, to be released from self. It is more common to use this word transcendence in reference to God. The word acknowledges that while God is knowable in his love for us, nonetheless his infinite love surpasses our comprehension. His transcendence is inseparable from the truth of his excess of love. Only love leads to a deeper knowledge that the God we seek is beyond our grasp. This knowledge of God, when it deepens in our soul, is always a knowing of him by more intense love. No other option of knowledge is possible after a certain point in the pursuit of God but to love him more deeply, surrendering ourselves to him. The experiential knowledge of God received by love is unlike any knowledge of things in this world. The knowledge of God in deeper prayer is a knowledge of being drawn to him by a love experienced in the depth of the soul. But for this love to take place, a transcendence toward ourselves must also be a dynamic movement within prayer. Perhaps we do not sense this necessity so easily. Yet there is an absolute spiritual need to leave ourselves, so to speak, in order to rest more securely in the One who is beyond ourselves. The ordinary sense of self has to be laid to rest and put aside; a release must take place. Prayer requires this "leave taking" from ourselves. Our attentiveness must concentrate on Someone else, an effort that is due, not primarily to mental discipline, but to love. Not that in prayer we lose consciousness of self completely and enter a strange world, but our attentiveness in love must depart from self and direct itself to a reality beyond ourselves.

～

Rather than making God remote and distant, beyond our capacity to know him, the truth of divine transcendence should urge our soul to seek him with a profound generosity. If God surpasses the reach of our desire and is beyond every yearning and aspiration, the only option is a self-giving that stretches us in increasing ways. Our self-giving must extend beyond our previous offerings in a progressive way. The hidden transcendence of God, once it is confronted by our soul, should provoke a great desire to pass beyond previous limits and hesitations in our self-giving. This compelling need of the soul may explain in part why saints literally poured out their lives for the sake of others. When the transcendence of God is engaged in a serious manner, in its implacable mystery and truth, his personal impact upon our soul demands that we give in ever greater sacrificial ways. The conviction of the personal presence of God as always elusive and hiding elicits this stretching of our life in generosity. Divine transcendence experienced as an essential hiddenness of God must be met by a response of generous self-offering. In souls taken up with a consuming love for God, the personal experience of God's concealment provokes the need to find concrete ways to please him that can become ever more creative in the circumstances of our lives.

~

A frustration of intelligence will accompany contemplative love to some degree. We should simply remember that this love receives its drive and impetus from a love infinitely beyond our capacity for knowledge. So much so that the disparity of love between the divine beloved and the human lover makes the effort to *understand* God's love an ultimately futile endeavor. Divine love has no ultimate words to describe it; no analogy or comparison provides adequate light. On the other hand, sometimes we may sense we are closer to this transcendent truth when we realize how incompatible notions seem to combine in the reality of God's love. An example might be the sacred vulnerability of God in his love despite his omnipotence in love. Likewise, in the experience of prayer itself: never in our prayer do we know what actually happens inside God himself when he draws near to us in his love. And yet we can sense the utterly personal nature of a gaze upon our soul and an exchange taking place at hidden depths of the soul. Indeed, the love in God can become almost a crushing truth in prayer, too overpowering for our soul. Rather than a comfort to our soul, divine love may prostrate us on some days in a helpless poverty and un-comprehending state. On these days, our soul can only close its eyes and stare in darkness at divine love. Even when Jesus is close in the near presence of a tabernacle, and we are certain of his presence and his love, this same presence of love stretches to distances that are immeasurable even within our own soul. We cannot take hold of the reality, as it were, and place it in front of us. The disproportion between his love and our meager awareness of his love is bound to intensify over time if we grow in contemplative graces. Indeed, it can be a failing in prayer to evade the incomprehension of his love, preferring instead to embrace images of God comfortable to our mind. It is the nature of deeper love in a contemplative life to take us down dark paths to unknown territories of what may seem a vacant blindness of mind. On a rare day, perhaps, the vast love we partially perceive is understood to exceed every possible thought. In its presence, we can only stammer or remain silent, with no other option. A kind of all-encompassing impoverishment of soul before God then becomes the only possible prayer.

∼

"However sublime may be the knowledge God gives the soul in this life, it is but like a glimpse of Him from a great distance" (Saint John of the Cross, *The Spiritual Canticle*). An awareness of God as transcendent, holy mystery, beyond the grasp of our immediate experience in prayer, may be a recurrent necessity in prayer. Yet this conviction does not oppose the desire for an encounter with God in prayer. We would not go to prayer if we did not seek such an encounter. But the safeguard of a genuine encounter with God in prayer is always to begin, continue, and end our time in prayer with the awareness that every possible experience of God surpasses our meager understanding. We cannot measure our experience of God in prayer as if there were reliable barometers for such a calculation. God knows what is in the deeper desire of the heart better than we can know. It is that deeper longing for him that is always the true measure of prayer. But this longing is often unknown to us in any direct manner because it resides at hidden depths within the soul. And for the sake of a pure intention in our prayer, and a greater purity of love, it is better that we do not examine this.

7

The Night Trials of
Contemplative Faith

It is such a bitter agony . . . seeing myself submerged in shadows without being able to make out the smallest glimmer of light, feeling a great abandonment from God and from absolutely everything, also a feeling within myself that everything has crumbled . . . and at the same time a thirst, without any hope of ever being satisfied, to love Our Lord immensely.

> —Saint Maria Maravillas of Jesus
>   (unpublished quotation, Brooklyn Carmel)

We cannot avoid this law of the spiritual life: that in order to come to the point where we can finally abandon ourselves totally *to* God, we must first feel what appears to be utter abandonment *by* God.

> —Erasmo Leiva-Merikakis, *Fire of Mercy*

The night of the spirit is the sign of the maturity of the soul. . . . Then one no longer lives on anything but the alms of unknown, inapprehensible grace.

> —Raïssa Maritain, *Raïssa's Journal*

The experiential paradox of contemplative prayer lies essentially in its combination of interior darkness undergone by the mind and intense desire inflaming the will. In both aspects, supernatural grace is operating. Deeper faith causes a greater obscurity in the mind toward truths of revelation, inasmuch as the soul embraces these truths from a closer vantage, as it were, savoring them in a certain blindness. Deeper love, on the other hand, draws the will in desire and longing for God. Both these effects are at work as a soul gives itself more fully to God. God is near and yet hidden, longed for and yet silent, present and yet concealed, exquisitely close and yet unreachable. The experience of darkness in contemplative prayer is perhaps the decisive test determining the soul's depth of desire for God. Those who love much do not allow this difficulty to deflect them from their path of love. "The mysticism of darkness comes about where love alone is able to see" (Joseph Ratzinger, Behold the Pierced One).

The descent of darkness upon the soul is a recurring image used to describe the experience of supernatural contemplation. Perhaps the image is not entirely helpful and is open to misinterpretations. Darkness seems to suggest a loss or weakening of faith. But the true contemplative experience, from its inception, has nothing to do with a reduced or fading faith. No uncertainty or doubt about doctrinal matters of belief is taking place. Quite the contrary, for a deeper embrace of revealed Christian truth necessarily undergirds the genuine contemplative night of faith. A soul does not receive the grace of contemplation unless it has advanced in the supernatural virtue of faith. It believes more intensely. What cannot be seen in vision it knows more surely by love as a presence, but now in greater obscurity, in the blind certitude of faith. Indeed, the divine presence draws a more piercing conviction from a deeper region of the soul inasmuch as love inflames a stronger desire for God. The intellect's desire to see with clarity may be vanquished in a certain sense, overcome in its capacity for comprehension. Yet at a deeper level of conviction in contemplative prayer, the soul possesses by means of love a more intense certainty of the divine presence. An experience of the drawing power of the divine will upon its own will is the reason for this certainty. God may be concealed from sight in the current darkness of an hour of prayer, but he is not hidden from the will's longing in love, despite the darkness that may envelop the mind. Ask the contemplatives if the darkness suppresses love or empties out desire. Just the opposite, they will say, for it is love itself that mysteriously conveys a knowledge of the One sought. Ask the contemplatives if the allure of the tabernacle diminishes when the shadows of darkness surround them. No, they will say, the unseen presence is more real than ever. The tabernacle in a special manner exercises a power of

presence that at times draws intense desire from a
depth within the soul.

~

What precisely, then, is this experience of the
"night" in a contemplative life? For, in fact, the
struggle with shifting light and darkness in prayer
is repetitive for many souls, and a rhythmic pattern
is frequently observed over the long course of years
of prayer. The periodic return of night and shadow
can be likened to a change in seasonal weather. A
soul, after enjoying for a time the comfort of God's
presence in prayer seems suddenly and without reason to lose its spiritual bond with God's presence,
as though an invisible hand let go and released it.
No longer secure and held, it now finds itself in
prayer walking a harder path into dim, shadowed
places within the soul. The silence of prayer may
get darker as the days continue despite a soul's desire for God. The companionship with God enjoyed earlier fades into a darker solitude in prayer.
Lost and alone, wandering in unfamiliar territory,
the soul may turn to silent prayer with a sense of
anxious foreboding. The image of darkness is an
apt metaphor for this recurrent experience. Without some understanding when this trial of prayer
is first undergone, it is very possible that confu-

sion overcomes the soul and impedes the actual invitation of deeper graces at work. The taste of darkness often indicates a transition in prayer and a need for greater trust, and it must not be misrepresented or interpreted falsely. Spiritual testimony abounds that painful darkness in prayer is not a descent into spiritual disability or loss. By no means is it a threatening moment, as though faith were edging toward a collapse that might occur without warning. On the contrary, the real movement taking place in the interior life is the entry into a greater hidden depth of soul. Perhaps the famous image of Plato's cave hints at the soul's contemplative experience in these patterns. The inability of the eyes to see inside a cave when it first leaves behind the sunlight is like the experience of darkness in contemplative life. The blindness of perception is an initial inability to adjust one's sight. The faculty of spiritual seeing is not accustomed yet to a more serious encounter with God, and for that reason it is overwhelmed. In contrast, the easier encounters with God of previous days may have been more superficial spiritual experiences by means of imagination and emotional comfort. The soul has begun, instead, to plunge into deeper waters in its relations with God.

~

"The true light shines in the darkness, but one must get accustomed to finding it there" (Augustín Guillerand, *They Speak by Silences*). Naturally, the metaphor of darkness does not draw us. On the contrary, it offers a forbidding prospect in the spiritual realm. It may sound like a form of spiritual illness is being identified, a condition that should be avoided by preventive measures and overcome as soon as possible. It seems to imply a mistake or error for which the soul can be at fault, a veering away, a detour from the right path. Darkness suggests the soul has wandered and lost its way, requiring some remedy. Nothing in the image invites an understanding that the entry into darkness is in fact a providential turn in the life of the soul. A great paradox of release for the soul hides in this metaphor, awaiting discovery. The truth may not be suspected until a particular insight takes place in prayer. The metaphor has to pass from a poetic image to an actual experience in prayer that contradicts the early impression of a downturn or backtracking in prayer. The great insight comes in realizing with deeper faith that the divine presence conceals itself in close proximity to the soul precisely *within* a sacred experience of darkness. The personal presence of God awaits us now in true intimacy under the cover of shadows. Only in a darkness where we cannot see in front of us is this

more intimate presence of the Lord encountered.
We must accept, by a simplicity of intense faith,
that God's divine presence hides quietly, mysteriously, underneath a steady darkness. A sharp insight of faith can open us to this truth at the heart
of silent interior prayer. The light is not seen, a
cloud covers us, yet Our Lord's personal presence
is close by, near us even in our blindness, piercing
the conviction of our interior being.

∼

In a somewhat strange manner, deeper faith may
bring a new form of questioning to our soul, perhaps not articulated so clearly, yet present at times
without our notice. The questioning regards the
unfamiliar path on which we find ourselves at times
stumbling in silent prayer. No one wants to turn
inadvertently down a byway or detour away from
God in prayer. And yet that worry sometimes rises
up when periods of a dry absence of satisfaction
take over the hours and days of prayer. Does God
hide only temporarily, or have we lost our way
at some point? The possibility that we may have
taken a mistaken turn while inattentive to the road
may place our soul in a state of anxiousness. Or
the questioning may have no concrete thought to
accompany it, no reason behind it. The presence

of anxiety in the heart can seem more like the presence of a solitary intruder who slipped in the door
when it was unbolted and now hides somewhere
inside. We should not trouble ourselves with examining any of this. The better approach is to ignore these reactions. The sign that God remains
near and continues to draw our soul is always the
unrelieved, steady hunger we experience in prayer.
The more deeply this hunger permeates the soul,
the more safely we walk in prayer. And the deeper
the hunger, the less it may be felt in any emotive
manner. The hunger is a passion for God in the
depths of the soul, often concealed. The one thing
that does matter in prayer is that we persevere in
that same passion for God when we sense inwardly
the desire for him. We have to persist in a prayer
of great need for God even without any felt sense
of a passion for God burning within the depths of
our soul. And often this is helped simply by putting
that desire into a short, evocative cry directed in
simple words to the heart of God.

∽

No soul should venture by some impulse of curiosity into the so-called contemplative nights of
faith, as if exploring the feel of darkness in prayer,
unsure of the outcome. Counterfeit versions of the

dark night of faith are not uncommon, and they are ill-advised. Mistakes in matters of faith are never of small issue; retracing one's steps may be no easy thing. Deliberate entry into doubt, indiscreet questioning of doctrines of faith, the indulged plunge of the mind into amorphous shadow, all these are dangerous departures from the true path of prayer. They have nothing to do with the contemplative night of faith, which is not sought by some kind of adventurous impulse. On the contrary, the genuine experience of contemplative darkness comes without a soul seeking it. It comes unexpectedly, by surprise, extended by the hand of God in pure gratuity, like all divine love. And that is in part why the darkness is a difficult trial in the interior life of prayer. There is nothing in the prior experience of prayer to provide a point of reference or comparison. And yet there is less rupture with previous experience than might be thought from an initial glance. For it is always true that God never invites us closer to himself unless this invitation comes with a personal cost. The true continuity of all deeper encounter with God has to be experienced in the conviction of faith. Supernatural faith does not wane in the night of faith but simply roots itself into deeper layers of the soul.

⌇

In a passage from his sixth stanza commentary of *The Spiritual Canticle* on the suffering of a soul as it draws closer to God, Saint John of the Cross speaks of the soul's pain in not knowing God more deeply despite having a greater intimacy of love with him. Only a kind of stammering knowledge of God accompanies this closer contact with him. What Saint John of the Cross calls a "touch of divinity" extended in love toward the soul only plunges it into further incomprehension of God's reality of infinite love. The deeper experience of divine love always has this trait, that it intensifies in a soul the sense of God's transcendent holiness in love. Saint John of the Cross refers to this encounter with God's absolute holiness of love as an experience of the "I-don't-know-what" of God. A form of cognizance takes place, but it cannot be contained in words. Even to call it a knowledge can be misleading, for a soul perceives nothing so particular in contact with his presence. In an inexpressible manner, the soul passes beyond a barrier, beyond a veil of mystery. It brushes up against the divine holiness of love, but then is taken no farther. The experience of divine love drawing the soul silences the mind then in a sacred and wordless admiration. There is no desire to speak afterward of this love, and no description is possible. An absence of words accompanies any recollection of the hour. A silence imbued with a deep longing for God's love is the only response a soul can carry away from this hour.

~

This passage from Saint John of the Cross is instructive for more than a comment on the deeper contemplative life of love. The reference to the "I-don't-know-what" of God can be extended to the entire realm of relations with God's will. God's actions in grace toward our souls are constant and providential, but they also exceed our comprehension in any present hour. We have to wait and allow the truth of divine providence to unfold its full mosaic of meaning. His will reveals itself less in the midst of immediate dramas, more in the quiet intermissions. The significance of events and experiences is uncovered over time as a testimony that he has indeed been present, quietly watching and intervening. If we are fortunate in grace, we perceive at times the evidence of converging lines that mysteriously link events and influences in our life to a wise, all-knowing hand of divine sovereignty shaping our life. We know then most certainly, but without knowing exactly how, that God has been mysteriously active in our life. We may have no clear explanation or understanding of this, but only an unshakeable conviction that God has left the unmistakable sign of his presence. Faith, when it intensifies in this manner, always brings us into contact with a God who is both very close at hand in love and acting in a way that "I-do-not-know" at the time.

~

It is interesting to observe the manner in which the Danish Protestant Søren Kierkegaard possibly approached aspects of a kind of contemplative faith. What Kierkegaard refers to paradoxically as "uncertainty" in the experience of faith is for him, not its lack of certainty as fact and reality, but rather the obscurity that can enclose the contents of faith, requiring a blind leap of faith. In a manner at times similar to the descriptions of Saint John of the Cross, he proposes that the believer's engagement with the truths of faith is not immune, on a personal level, to shadows and darkness despite the firmness and intensity of faith. As Saint John of the Cross affirms more emphatically, the intensity of faith will even accentuate to some degree the experience in prayer of obscurity and darkness within the mind. For both men, this subjective experience does not undermine what is believed. The darkness experienced simply accompanies more intense faith. Indeed, Saint John of the Cross affirms that it is a condition for a deeper experience in faith of transcendent truths that they should stretch beyond the capacity of the human mind. Kierkegaard might have gained much by reading Saint John of the Cross, the great Catholic commentator on experiential darkness in the spiritual life. The teaching of Saint John of the Cross is profound and necessary: the soul confronted and overcome by infinite transcendent truth, yet still inflamed with an intense passion for God. For both men, faith is an intensely personal act precisely when all becomes darkness to the eyes of faith. Saint John of the Cross, blessed by the gift of the personal presence of Jesus Christ in the Eucharist, finds his answer in the purifying path of self-emptying love for the Beloved, which makes the hours of blindness resonate with hidden luminosity. Even in darkness, the concealed presence of the Beloved known in faith's certitude can become a passion of love consuming the desire of the soul.

～

All advancement in contemplative grace is tied directly to the response of the will in its love for God and his will despite any experience of darkness. Inasmuch as the soul gives itself in prayer to a more intense desire to be one with the will of God, it may seem to plunge into a deeper interior darkness. This is a surprising paradox, since we would expect the comfort of a richer companionship with the presence of God when love for God's will is clearly sought and then chosen in actions. The result contradicts, certainly, human expressions of love. But we have to set our mind on divine things and not on human things. God takes the soul into a greater purification in contemplative graces precisely by means of love. It is as though he watches the response of the soul when it suffers darkness, awaits our reaction to the call to serve him in darkness, observes our attention to love's details while we walk in darkness. Now when we go to prayer, we may find it is only love itself that we desire, not to dwell with our mind on reflections or in pursuit of spiritual insights. The quiet of an absorbed, loving attention to God even when all is darkness becomes the exclusive impulse attracting our soul. The darkness that may have intimidated us earlier now becomes a familiar setting for prayer, its discomfort no longer a concern. The desire of the soul is simply to give itself in love to God and his will. On some days, the certainty of his presence in a depth of the soul allows that desire to remain inflamed without apparent effort. On those days, the darkness itself seems inseparable from his presence, a hiding place for his love, as though our inner eyes had finally opened to a truth that had been all along present.

∼

For some souls the "experiential" confirmation of the doctrine of the divine indwelling in the soul involves the taste of extreme poverty at the depth of the soul. It may seem to offer nothing disclosing an encounter with the divine. In these people, God does not favor the soul with a consoling experience of himself when he offers intimacy to the soul. Rather, at a level of deep personal awareness, the soul awakens gradually to its true nothingness. The taste of its own emptiness and absolute need before God becomes a vivid, undeniable fact and, indeed, a crushing truth on certain days when the soul has become like an ignored beggar. It may be that in these souls the intensifying diminishment of self is a necessity for a greater intimacy with God. A pattern begins to show in their lives. While certain of God's presence mysteriously at work within them, these souls in prayer find themselves often alone and wretchedly empty. Only in an abject poverty do the divine encounters occur. It is not an elevation the soul undergoes then but a further death within itself. New desires for the offering and loss of itself take shape subsequently. At some inaccessible depth within the soul, it longs for an annihilation of self in the offering of love. The desire lingers as a demand for some essential abnegation that has no concrete resolution but, nonetheless, seems to fill the soul. It is as though the indwelling presence of God within them were urging a prostration of spirit before a God who now seemed less known than ever.

~

The experience of interior darkness in prayer teaches another lesson. Our nothingness is felt more vividly, more tangibly, when darkness encloses our interior life. In groping blindly, stumbling our way through shadows, we can seem in prayer like specks of dust floating in an infinitely vast universe. The darkness when it thickens makes us small and insignificant, almost to the point of disappearing. We become unimportant to ourselves in this night of darkness, insubstantial and weightless, as it were. It may take time to understand such darkness as a benefit to the soul, which is to help us forget ourselves. In turning our eyes from self, we gaze, not into a vast night, but blindly toward a real presence within us and, beyond us, toward a real person who is the Lord Jesus himself. The nothingness of ourselves is not important; the presence of Our Lord takes our desire captive. The darkness becomes an interior place where our own nothingness can join company with another who is present. He is unseen and we are blind, yet he is known as present to us, probing and reaching more deeply into us with love.

~

The release after her death of letters written by Mother Teresa concerning her decades-long trial of interior darkness shocked even the sisters of her congregation. It seems that no one suspected this dimension in her life. She gave no hint outwardly of grave interior suffering in her relations with God in prayer. Yet it should not be so surprising in retrospect that God may choose a Gethsemane of interior suffering in drawing a saint to a greater offering for souls. She herself would respond after a time with a deeper awareness of her union with the Passion of Our Lord through this trial, writing in 1958 (*Come Be My Light*): "When you asked to imprint Your Passion on my heart—is this the answer? . . . If souls are brought to You—if my suffering satiates Your Thirst—here I am, Lord, with joy I accept all to the end of my life—& I will smile at Your Hidden Face—always." What is not so well known is that Mother Teresa was helped in 1961 by an insight of a Belgian Jesuit priest in India, Father Joseph Neuner. His words did not lift from her this painful interior trial, but they presented an understanding that every soul should embrace in a trial of darkness. And surely to have a sense of meaning and purpose that God is at work is the great insight we need in all suffering. Father Neuner simply asked Mother Teresa to consider the possibility that God wanted her, not just to serve in generosity the poorest of the poor, but to be herself one of the *poorest* of the poor; that this trial of darkness was in God's plan to unite her with a poverty she had not realized yet in life, that she was to become one with her poor in a manner she had not understood yet. Her letters of darkness diminish markedly after this exchange with Father Neuner.

~

No one seeking God should fear the storms that may submerge the soul for a time but that can never take God from us. The darkness can have variations, combining external trials in life with interior hardship in prayer. It would seem that God displays his artistic hand in unusual ways when he works on bringing a soul along a road that leads to true holiness. Inevitably he strips these souls, taking from them their various mannered accoutrements of piety and spiritual habit and casting it all away in the rubbish heap. He likewise might undermine their health, their reputation, their enjoyments, even their love for himself when it conceals egoistic tendencies. Yet somehow, with a strength and resilience that is not their own, most who begin to taste contemplation do not falter. They stay on the path. Nothing crushes their conviction of a mysterious, invisible companionship hiding in events of costly self-emptying. In many cases, their sureness of God's presence seems to thrive even more when there is no evidence for their certitude. After a while the "seasoned contemplatives" will say they have lived too long in his presence, too long observing his departures and his returns, to trouble now with needless questions about God's doings in their regard.

∼

The contemplative experience of the night of faith displays a consistent benefit—a great solidity of soul, firm and unshakeable in its conviction of God. The experience is rooted in a deep certitude of God as a hidden presence within the soul and known in love. As the soul adjusts itself to shadows as the hiding place for its rendezvous with God, it is no longer troubled by darkness. When we are in prayer, the personal presence of God elicits an ease of love and a simple and uncomplicated conviction, no longer subject to unstable feeling or fluctuations of awareness. This same certitude of his presence feeds a steady longing for God that requires no real effort on the soul's part, only a step into the quiet of interior desire. That flame of longing for God is typically never extinguished once it has been lit. It may not be felt always, but its presence even when unfelt burns in a deeper region of the soul, where our will meets the will of God. All this is not chosen by our soul, never the result of an exploration in curiosity, never a venturing into supposed deeper waters. Rather, a surrender to love inflames the soul in the night of faith. This act of surrender is never entirely under our own control, but rather a submission to another who is drawing us. It takes place as a deeper impulse of soul beneath any conscious thought, as though we were swept forward in the movement of a tide.

8

The Desert of Deeper Prayer

Give me a man in love: he knows what I mean. give
me one who yearns; give me one who is hungry;
give me one far away in this desert, who is thirsty
and sighs for the spring of the Eternal country.
Give me that sort of man: he knows what I mean.
But if I speak to a cold man, he just does not know
what I am talking about.

> —Saint Augustine,
> *Tract. in John, 26.4*

Few there are with the knowledge and desire for
entering upon this supreme nakedness and emptiness of spirit. . . . This is a venture in which God
alone is sought and gained, thus only God ought
to be sought and gained.

> —Saint John of the Cross,
> *The Ascent of Mount Carmel*

A man in a desert can hold absence in his cupped
hands knowing it is something that feeds him more
than water.

> —Michael Ondaatje,
> *The English Patient*

Prayer requires courage not to halt on the long journey. Underlying all serious prayer is the certitude of a presence sought, even when it is unseen, unfelt, veiled in obscurity. Once the presence of Our Lord has been met, the life of prayer burns with a quiet flame that is never extinguished. We may persevere through periods of unrewarding effort in the silence of seeking God. We may enter an interior desert of the soul that seems to cast sand and debris upon all our longing for God. We walk blindly, unhesitatingly, not waylaid by discouragement, but turned to the horizon of a presence of mystery before our darkened gaze. We come to know his presence in a far deeper certitude inasmuch as we allow him to lead our way. He is present always, with his eyes upon us, even when it seems we are blind and alone. Those who cross a threshold of deeper conviction in prayer know with certainty a depth of his presence that undergirds every hour of shadowed prayer. "The further you go into the desert, the closer you come to God" (an Arabic proverb).

Souls anxious for a rescue in prayer when darkness descends upon them may have a hard time in silent prayer. The darkness goes with the territory; the shades cannot be evaded. For most people committed to a serious practice of silent prayer, interior bouts of confusion and heaviness are seasonal recurrences. At times these experiences may seem to throw a battering ram against the soul, requiring some form of defensive posture. In rarer cases, the shadows converge from different directions as though posing a threat to faith itself. Most often, however, the reality of darkness in the interior life has no such intense drama. Trials of this sort come periodically, with predictable regularity, but the experience is consistent with other trials in the spiritual life. Trials of every kind are temporary, a matter of patient endurance. Trials in the interior life of prayer are no different. They can be painful in the way that a sharp bone injury is painful, aching with every movement. Yet nothing of such pain is insurmountable. Every interior trial simply asks us to cross a threshold more deeply into the mysterious presence of God within our soul.

∼

"The desert loves to strip bare" (Saint Jerome). There is no need to examine the desert trial in prayer, as though looking for an answer that would make it disappear. Analysis does not help; seeking remedies brings no relief. It is better to keep the longer view in sight. On some days, the decisive choice to remain in prayer is all that matters. The choice to stay in prayer, not to leave whatever the cost, to suffer even humiliation in prayer, may sound to some people like a stubborn mania. But this refusal to give up in prayer is often a sign of a serious love in prayer. When prayer seems nothing but forced exertion, a sweating strain and struggle, when departing from prayer would be like relief from an unbearable cramp, a deep impulse of love may often hide in the effort simply to remain. Indeed, our desire for God *in his eyes* may be most intense in prayer when we are shackled and overcome with difficulty. Unknown desires of the soul are present in prayer that we cannot verify for ourselves. The important thing is never to lose this conviction of the unseen truth of prayer. Let us rejoice, then, if that is possible, when the sacred hour costs us. Any impulse to abandon prayer must be renounced. A prayer devoid of feeling, yet endured to the finish, often conceals a great longing for God. The hour may offer no comfort, no satisfaction or joy, just vacancy in our heart and soul. At best, we may think we have shown only spiritual discipline, enduring an exercise that has stretched tautly the fibers of our heart. But let us not confuse heaviness of spirit with an absence of love. Perhaps we love most in prayer when we suffer our prayer. The love for God that we do not experience often burns quietly then at secret depths in our soul.

~

"You enter God's apprenticeship only by persevering in prayers that are not answered" (Antoine de Saint-Exupéry, in Erasmo Leiva-Merikakis, *Fire of Mercy*). The uncertainty of the soul in a condition of interior darkness ordinarily involves a taste of diminished spiritual confidence, as though God no longer paid attention to its cry of need. The soul feels stripped and emptied, without apparent reason, of any favor in God's eyes. That is a great suffering to a soul that has earlier enjoyed a sense of strong love from God, and it has to be endured to some degree in all contemplative lives. Yet for a soul standing on the edge of this abyss of uncertainty, unsure of God's love, the hour is ripe for a great leap of faith and a deeper entry into the reality of love. Perhaps the true depth of God's love is not encountered until we pass through a prolonged, helpless need for him. The release that comes to a soul when it finally accepts the embrace of darkness as the hiding place of divine favor will take a soul beyond any previous conviction of being loved by God.

～

We ought in prayer to pay it no mind: a dry tongue, a heart burnt and empty, thoughts frozen and unmoving, will not keep us from speaking words of love. We should ignore the discomfort and trust we will find the few phrases we need. The conditions of silent prayer can often seem unfavorable. But let us forget the appearance and plunge beneath

the empty feeling. A parched soul can pronounce
very rich words of love. Words spoken from deep
within the soul do not need the support of emotion. Language has no restraint, no limitation, in
these deeper desert regions of the soul. The words
require only a conviction that the Beloved hears
them. The great need is often simply to push on
through the desert of aridity even as the dry ex-
panses seem to extend beyond sight. What is discovered in due time is that these desert stretches are
not an unbroken ordeal and trial of tiring heat. The
days at certain hours are fed by a cool breeze that
refreshes entirely by surprise. Let us know with
certainty in prayer that every desert has its hidden
springs, and this is true as well in the desert of the
soul. The silent oasis of a deep longing for God is
like a spring in the desert, where words are given to
us in prayer without our seeking them. Our soul
speaks them unaware of the concealed love that
hides in a few spare words. We may only realize
the deeper truth later: without knowing their destination, these words make their way across vast
stretches in the inner soul and arrive at the heart
of our Beloved.

～

We risk losing the attraction for silent prayer if we
indulge the thought that God is no longer listen-

ing to us in that silence. The troubling thought can take hold that he has departed, has left the room, as it were, as though he had tired of us and lost interest. Sometimes this mistake has its origin in looking upon the mystery of God as a terrible barrier to knowing him. The thought may occur that it is only a wishful yearning we have that he hears us in prayer, with nothing to assure us. We may stare too fixedly at the lack of any sign of his presence. The bodily senses may ache for a confirmation of his presence and rebel against the need to sustain our faith in simplicity of mind and heart. In all this we have to face the real dilemma and deeper task of prayer. Living our faith in silent prayer often means to mortify a desire for some physical attestation of his presence. His presence in silence soaks us in mystery, but we do not realize this truth at times. Perhaps we must simply allow the quiet to do its part, for the gift of silence is clearly desired by God as a means of mysterious communication with himself. The silence is capable of permeating our soul, making us forget our own need. In faith we must know that Our Lord is there in the silence, especially near a tabernacle. He allows our heart to be touched in silence, without a need for words. He listens more than we realize to the silence within our heart. In a mysterious way, the silence deepens in its effect when our longing for him is more intense. In a greater depth of silence, our longing for him stretches toward his presence even when we do not know this. Although he remains concealed in mystery, there is no barrier separating us from him.

~

"What do my tastes matter, O Lord, for me there is nothing more than thyself" (Saint Teresa of Avila, in Jacques and Raïssa Maritain, *Prayer and Intelligence*). A threshold has perhaps been crossed without our realizing it when our sense of closeness to God in prayer finds itself displaced and fractured by a sudden inability to get near his hidden presence. None of this signifies a departure of God or a loss of his presence to our soul. On the contrary, the experience may be due precisely to an intense desire for his presence that for a time has been consuming our soul. After years of commitment to prayer, when we already yearn with some intensity for God, we may find that interior darkness hiding a concealed God has become the customary setting for prayer. The encounter with God in prayer is wrapped in the obscurity of shadows. It is as though all the lights had to be turned off and a room plunged into darkness to realize his actual presence more securely. This is an interior truth of the soul, not a matter literally of an external ambiance. Once we accustom ourselves to this interior condition of prayer, blindness to some degree becomes a steady companion in our silent prayer. Apparently, it is a necessary blindness if we are to see one day the face of our crucified Lord, and it is not dissipated by any effort on our part. It has to be accepted and embraced as a blessing inasmuch as it hides the presence of Our Lord in greater mystery.

~

The blindness is difficult to bear, especially when we are not yet accustomed to it. A natural revulsion takes place in us at the inability to "see" in prayer beyond a single step ahead. At times our mind in confusion may reach out impulsively as though to grasp at any object of thought, anything to hold as a temporary interest. We may find ourselves groping for steadiness, stumbling and tripping, unsure of what to seek in prayer. It is easy at first to think we have lost God in some permanent way, that we will be alone. The sense of God's departure, the loss of his presence, weighs on the interior spirit. It may feel some days as though a film of opaqueness were coating the soul, a heavy covering that constrains the mind and heart. But this is not the truth of what is happening in prayer. The darkness may seem to confirm the disappearance of God, or perhaps his displeasure with our soul, his frustration at our lack of love for him. But this thought is a lie and deception, and the dark whispers must be repudiated. Instead, we must find our way in the darkness to the center of our soul as best we can with a new cultivation of certitude. A pure faith must stretch itself inwardly where *his* secret presence hides. The certitude of his concealed presence beyond inner barriers that we have not yet crossed is what alone may keep us in an abiding security. Indeed, the certitude allows us to gain much even while suffering darkness in prayer. The calm conviction must be that on the far side of this darkness, the Beloved hides, waiting for our soul. In fact, we can anticipate his coming closer in this darkness precisely by means of our certitude. In effect, we must allow his hand to take our own and lead us while we are seeing nothing. When he comes, his arrival will not be perceived. But soon we may hope to know this truth of his immediate presence more certainly. He loves the souls who gaze with unseeing eyes at his secret presence within their own dark silence. And he answers their longing with an inevitable assurance that it is only a short time in this life that keeps them apart from him.

~

Perhaps love surges up within our soul precisely at the hour of prayer when we seem to ourselves caged in the dark corners of our heart's discontent. Our own perception of prayer is never the deeper truth of prayer. Shadows befogging our mind, jagged emotion disturbing our calm, thoughts agitated and restless, these adverse conditions do not prevent the offering of our soul to God. The actual unseen truth is that God at the core of our being gazes upon the deeper, hidden reality of our soul. He knows well that no one pursues him steadily without a profound desire and need for him. What is necessary above all is to seek a depth of love in prayer. The soul that returns steadily despite enduring repeated pain in prayer often has deep layers of concealed hunger and love. When we do not give up despite what seems harshness and difficulty in prayer, we pronounce to God our wordless hunger for him. Let us take heart and understand this truth correctly. Dust on our lips, a weary, weighed-down heart, a mind unable to think a clear thought—these symptoms may appear to be an impossible hindrance to prayer. Perhaps, on the contrary, they are rather the marks of poverty in prayer, not at all a lack of love in prayer. The poverty has a definite purpose in the interior life, which is to take our soul slowly to a purer need for God, into regions of the soul where a hunger deeper and more concealed still awaits us.

∽

If in prayer we search in earnest, we may discover something more significant than a sonorous sound.

We encounter anew the great truth at the heart of prayer—the One who is addressed in prayer. The holy presence of God hiding in prayer begins to show itself, and then a curtain lifts, changing everything. On that day, the spoken words of prayer seem as if to elevate and climb over a wall, carrying the soul into an inner chamber where a different communication now becomes possible. All becomes new in that interior location. An awareness crystallizes that God is in truth present, listening to words and to the soul's silence. This realization of Our Lord's actual presence alters prayer irrevocably. Words that for years were staid and lifeless are now directed toward a destination in the heart of God. It is as though a flame had come alive inside the words and a wind were stirring the flame. The words quicken and pause interchangeably, suggesting and urging, identifying a need to be pursued, an insight to be protected. On a given day, particular words or phrases may seem strangely in union with the silence at the center of prayer. Yet the silence itself may be stronger than any spoken words. The words enlivened by the strength of silence seem to return quietly to the heart once they are spoken. And sometimes the sound of words subsides with a clean finality, and we know only an unchanging presence in the silence for a brief time after the words have finished.

~

Over many years, souls of serious prayer hold firm through the dark passageways of silence, stumbling blindly at times with labored steps and an outstretched hand, but never stopping, moving always toward the One who is present but not seen. Each day of silent prayer is a departure for a destination without markers, with no clear measure of progress, without a point of lasting arrival. Nonetheless, while a path of recurring obstacles must be walked, deeper prayer is not a matter primarily of "crisis management" directed to interior trials in prayer. It is much more the simplicity of a patient waiting, of a receptive capacity before God's mysterious design upon our life, which includes the journey through interior darkness. The essential *truth* of prayer, even in the dark hours of struggle, is an encounter with the *mystery* of divine presence, with the One who is met in faith, a presence that recedes and hides, and then once again returns. We do not have to travel far distances to the rendezvous with his loving presence. It can happen at any time, anywhere, even plunged in shadows. What is necessary is a more basic task. We have to quiet our restless desire to draw his presence in mystery down to a familiar recognition. We must let God be God in his mystery of love. Only then, perhaps, do we realize sometimes how close he has been to us all along. Prayer is not meant to be a search for a location where we finally find God, where we can now *have* God in a way of that was not possible previously. It is, rather, an entry into a secret intensity of loving, into a place of pure conviction in the soul where all along he has been waiting to meet us.

∼

"Just as you enter this church building, so God wishes to enter your soul, for he promised: *I shall live in them, and I shall walk the corridors of their hearts*" (Saint Caesarius of Arles, in *The Liturgy of the Hours*). It is of course not difficult to affirm mentally the presence of God within us when that belief does not seem to ask anything more from us. It is much harder to embrace his personal presence within us in pure faith as a need in silent prayer, and this is the real demand in the time of darkness. A blind certitude of his personal presence must be cultivated in times of darkness. This acceptance of his presence can become something like an acquired taste, a taste not without some unpleasant quality to it. But this same certitude is the protection against discouragement in the difficult times of prayer. His presence can be fully embraced as a surrender of our mind in prayer. As we receive the grace to remain calm in the darkness of silent prayer, we will come to know his truth shining in this darkness. The presence of Our Lord, near to us, intensifies the mystery of his concealment. The sense of his concealment may often become a kind of predominant inner ambiance in the life of prayer. And yet an unfailing certitude of his concealed presence, a calm engagement in silence with *him in his hiding*, even when we are utterly blind, unable to see anything, slowly deepens. The darkness assumes less and less importance. Prayer in that silence becomes the consuming certitude that *he* is present, that his direct and immediate gaze rests on secret depths within our soul.

~

Silence of thought is not an absence of mental activity. The mind in contemplative prayer does not cease to exist because no particular thought occupies it. Would we say, for instance, that a lake vanishes when the water is completely still and not a trace of movement disturbs its surface? In fact, a lake has a special attraction and beauty just then. On a clear summer day without a breeze, a motionless lake exudes a pure beauty. Like a wet sheet of glass in the bright sunlight, it seems to gaze at the sky and receive a purity from above. Our mind in prayer can be like that when it is poised in silent attentiveness. Plunged in silence, undisturbed by distraction, our mind in contemplative prayer can enjoy an alert repose and deepen in a receptive quality. The absence of thought in that silence is not at all an emptiness of mind. While there may be no particular thoughts, nonetheless a longing for God may permeate our awareness in a noticeable way. When it is strongly felt, this longing resembles almost a silent presence within our soul. And the mind reflects this presence of desire within the soul just as a lake in sunlight mirrors the sky.

~

"It has been so long since I have spoken to You without effort, with the natural flow of a conversation that is never interrupted" (Maurice Blondel in Erasmo Leiva-Merikakis, *Fire of Mercy*). It is not possible to believe with intensity and evade at times an insecurity about God. While a kind of quasi-belief in God may settle for a dry thought drawing no real desire from a soul, anyone who believes intensely comes to know that God is a *person* not known so quickly. In a way, he is like someone easier to know while observing him from afar than by standing close and looking in his eyes. Gazing more directly provokes a sense of a barrier, even a distance, that cannot be overcome. All this may elicit at times a kind of a spiritual uncertainty, but one that can be fruitful for the deeper life of faith and prayer. The insecurity of soul aroused by our desire for him in his hiddenness has nothing to do with doubt. It is rather the uncertainty how he will make his presence known on any particular day. Only a more intense faith provokes and suffers this tension of soul. It becomes a repeated and steady experience in prayer.

~

Undergirding our profession of faith must be a recognition that God has granted a *gift* to us in our desire for him, even if we have no way to measure this desire or to express it adequately in words. And joined with this recognition must be a certainty in faith that God is moved by our desire for him, even if it seems we have no reliable evidence of this truth other than our certainty of it. After a while, however, we should make a discovery. The desire we have for God is inseparable from the gift of his presence to us. The desire is itself a sign of his presence, like a fragrance of beauty discerned in the vicinity of fresh roses, even if we do not see the rosebush. We would not desire him unless he was mysteriously close. And all the time we long for him within ourselves, it must be as well that we delight the heart of God. When we are drawn in desire to him, it is his love for us that is drawing our desire. This gift of our desire for him does not require a particular feeling but only that our soul be receptive in its longing for him. Indeed, the most effective desire in prayer seems always to rise up from a hidden depth of soul that we never realize exists until we begin to experience a deeper longing in ourselves for God. This can also happen at times in a surprising way outside prayer during the course of a day, in a manner similar to the sudden onset of strong physical hunger. As with all love, the deeper longing of a soul for God will never agree to being confined within limited times and secure places.

∼

We can assume that a very strong desire for God felt in prayer is due to God casting his gaze upon our soul in that hour. The desire is strong because the divine gaze draws from us this longing. We do not see his presence or the gaze of his eyes, but our longing for him is stirred because he is near and is looking at us. The proximity of his eyes, even when they are hidden, provokes our soul's desire for him. The more we realize in faith this link between our desire and his real presence and gaze, the more we come to perceive another truth of prayer. Seeking God in prayer is inseparable from a desire to disappear from ourselves under the gaze of those eyes, to lose all concern for ourselves and attend only to him. In this manner, our desire for God becomes a purer love for him at those hours when we are no longer aware of our desire. Then we love him without a thought of receiving something for ourselves. We want only to give ourselves to him, and this we do without effort. And in that desire for him alone, we may receive hidden gifts that we realize only in their effects after prayer. The primary gift is always a longing to offer ourselves more completely to him by offering ourselves in turn for other souls.

9

Contemplatives and Their Poverty

O Lord, give me all that leads me to You.
O Lord, take everything that diverts me from You.
O Lord, wrest me from myself and give me wholly
   to You.

—Saint Edith Stein,
Thoughts

There is no companionship which affords comfort
to the soul that longs for God; indeed, until she
finds Him everything causes greater solitude.

—Saint John of the Cross,
The Spiritual Canticle

In the thickets in Arabia you will lodge. . . . To the
thirsty bring water, meet the fugitive with bread.

—Isaiah 21:13–14

*The category of hidden souls we call contemplatives has
nothing to do with the external features of their lives.
What rather distinguishes them is their deeper offering to
God when the cross confronts them. Their hidden union
with God in love when facing trial is pronounced and*

strong, and typically well concealed. God seems to have a special love not only for these souls, but also for hiding their presence in the midst of crowds. His particular solicitude with contemplative souls is like a teacher or tutor with favorite pupils. He walks with them in their struggles and conceals his own hiddenness inside the obscurity of their lives. The contemplatives carry the presence of God in their souls in the way that a small country chapel with the Blessed Sacrament contains the presence of Almighty God. It seems in many cases that God is unusually protective of his choice to keep them in hiding. And he hides within them precisely through the trials that uniquely form their lives. "There are countless souls who possess God who derive no pleasure from that fact" ([Augustín Guillerand], They Speak by Silences*).*

Trials are bound to accompany every spiritual life. The mere mention of them is enough sometimes to arouse fear and hesitation in souls. The reality is not so intimidating, however, if we consider that trial and testing are always present in human life and ought to be necessary for any soul who is passionate in seeking God. The greater surprise would be that a closeness to God could come easily in our lives. The tests that ensue in a deeper contemplative life are subtle and often not considered prior to their arrival. Patterns do emerge, however, and it seems that many souls undergo similar types of trials. God is clearly seeking a purification

of the soul's desire for him, an emptying of egoism, through all so-called testing. Nonetheless, in
all contemplative lives there is a unique element in
the experience of trials. A wide variation of testing is evident. In many cases, the life is taken to
a greater obscurity, enhancing the sense of a soul
that it belongs to God alone. In all this we must
perceive the love of God in challenging our soul
to a greater faith and surrender of ourself.

~

Mysteriously, uniquely, yet predictably, contemplative souls are led by holy instincts of obedience
to a union with the cross. For a contemplative,
obedience to God is inseparable from love itself,
love for Jesus Christ crucified. Over a lifetime, that
truth becomes evident and indisputable. Surrender
to God in love does not permit exemption from this
spiritual law. But we should ponder more deeply
what kind of obedience animates the contemplative soul. This is an obedience of intense attraction,
not of duty or obligation. Obedience for contemplatives is like the inner compulsion of an artist
drawn to hours of hard work by a fever of love for
creating things of beauty. No true artist will say he
trudges to work in reluctance and distaste, forcing
his soul to the task. Contemplatives are similar in
their response. In a sense they recognize the cross

almost like their chosen art; no more to be evaded or refused than an artist running from the sight of beauty rising before his eyes. For all of us, the circumstances that bring crosses into our lives are rarely foreseen. But if we desire a more contemplative life, every hint of a new cross emerging in our lives should arouse a desire to surrender again in loving submission to the crucified Beloved on the cross.

～

The spirit of obedience in a contemplative is essentially a desire to complete a work of love. It is a disposition that affects day-to-day living. This impulse is very different from mere submission to orders or commands, which often means simply to be done with a task quickly and efficiently. The latter response may answer an obligation, fulfill a duty, finish a work, but it lacks the most important need. There is no personal gift made to another. This kind of obedience closes the will in narrowly upon the burden of some demand. It has no real generosity, even as it may claim faithfulness. The contemplative in obeying has a quite different interior awareness. There is a spiritual depth in the response. Obedience becomes a chance to express in action a personal love for the Beloved who has commanded. The real action takes place, not in completing a task, but in a personal choice to offer a gift to another. The action of any kind is a re-lease of love for the contemplative, energizing and expanding the soul. The submission becomes an act of embracing the beloved in an awareness of his love for that soul. And the soul by long habit recognizes this love of the beloved.

~

There are many variations of suffering in a contem-plative life, some easier to bear, others of a long duration. But in contemplatives, a gratitude is ex-tended toward all these visits of the cross, even when the struggles are protracted and difficult. At some point in a contemplative life, gratitude to God for the presence of a cross becomes a demand of love itself. This is so because a realization changes everything: the cross compels an irresistible need to offer one's love again to a Beloved. In the op-portunity to offer in love to the One loved, these souls are grateful. The cross itself in its pain is not their preoccupation. They perceive the deeper truth that it is not chance or coincidence but di-vine providence that chooses for them each cross and trial. They refuse to demur or balk at the di-vine intervention. On the contrary, their love is provoked, which is why obedience in that hour is not a burdensome choice. Their submission in love replicates the pattern of obedience in Christ's own life, which took him swiftly, more quickly than we realize, to the hill of Calvary. Contemplative lives may not move so fast as Christ's life took him to the cross. Nonetheless, it is inevitable that they should conclude their pilgrimage of obedience only by arriving at their own Calvary.

～

A sudden thunderstorm on an open country road with no shelter in sight, no option but to push heavily through gusting wind and sheets of rain, fighting through the violent summer deluge, not halting. Sometimes in circumstances of testing, there is no mapping out a plan and strategy. We must simply walk forward and raise our face to the hour. And who can say what abrupt storms in life await us for which we cannot prepare? Few trials of serious magnitude can be anticipated adequately, including the trials of interior prayer. They can be swift in their descent upon our lives, with no warning until the thunder is crashing overhead and lightning is splitting the sky. If pounding rains sweep in from nowhere and lash us blindly, so that we can hardly see a step ahead, we must not falter but walk even without a road in sight, certain that every storm passes eventually and that the sun hidden over the distant hills will break through a blackened horizon with new, ever more radiant light.

～

"Isn't this the great tragedy, to battle against God and not to be vanquished?" (Simone Weil, *Gravity and Grace*). It is perhaps not unusual for a contemplative soul to come to an intuitive realization that a divine action during the course of life has been slowly, deliberately shredding the soul, paring it down, emptying it, all with a clear purpose and plan. No longer do the trials and struggles of life seem to be isolated episodes independent of each other. Rather, they seem at a certain point joined in a unity, as though they fit as pieces into a single tapestry. They converge as one and coalesce in a meaning of deeper significance. The intuition gathers strength that the purpose of all suffering and trial has been to offer the soul up to God. A deep, inarticulate sense crystallizes that one's life has been chosen precisely for such an offering—a complete and total offering to God. This offering is perhaps not so much a voluntary undertaking by a soul out of love for God. The offering is understood to be the choice of God himself, who has been chipping away and sculpting in order to bring the soul gradually into a state of victimhood offered to him. The soul comes to perceive this truth with an undeniable certitude. Now, with an understanding of its true privilege, the soul receives a grace to embrace these numerous hidden ways of being offered more fully, come what may.

~

It would seem common to most contemplative
lives that they cannot avoid occasional struggles
with self-questioning and inner uncertainty. These
interludes of dark instability are a mystery of trial
and suffering that cannot be explained and yet are
evident in these lives. They are not a thing a soul
causes by some personal failure or negligence. And,
precisely for that reason, they are not something to
be feared. They descend as periods of trial upon
contemplative souls without warning, like winter
days covering the sun and bringing cold and chill
to the air. Some people look on a passage through
any inner darkness of soul as an impossible contra-
diction to a blessed life with God. The notion of
darkness seems incompatible with the clean, un-
obstructed vision of an untroubled faith. In fact,
great offerings of a soul often come only after a
time of a lingering, involuntary insecurity about
our relations with God. The idea of closeness to
God may acquire a new understanding when it is
no longer propped up and supported by steady experiences of spiritual comfort.

~

It can be surprising in a cloistered convent to see a
young face, usually fresh, animated, bright, with-
draw for no apparent reason into a private unease,

empty of its customary shine. Why this tentative, halting appearance in someone ordinarily full of light? Perhaps she is not so convinced of the life she has chosen? Doubt or indecision is not likely to be the case at all. Hard reality in dedicated religious settings can lay bare a soul's interior struggles despite every effort of self-concealment. These women of the cloister who are passionate to give themselves in love to God are at risk of interludes of self-exposure. Their single-mindedness for God makes them at times not so adept at hiding, especially in the early years of cloistered life. The dark confusion they may experience at times in the secrecy of prayer may leak out from the time of prayer. No words are necessary, no dramatic display need take place; the face alone reveals the unwanted distress. In corridors and refectories, at a stove or turning from a kitchen sink, a soul's anguish to give itself in love when feeling empty of love can be impossible to hide. It is a burden of communal religious life unknown to those beyond those walls. The serious souls soon enough realize and catch on. They learn the art of concealment beneath a steadily cheerful demeanor and thereby become more solitary in their interior life. The choice may be a lonely one, without human comfort, but over time it is a source of strength and a form of heroism in those on the way to a real depth of holiness.

~

In some lives, God leaves no surer mark of his great love over a lifetime than a slow branding of the heart. These souls are not customarily recognized by others in their closeness to God, nor perhaps do they realize it themselves. They live their hidden relationship with God's presence in their hours of prayer as though it were the most ordinary thing. The noise and bustle of cities is sometimes their hiding place, where it is quite easy to be anonymous among crowds. At first glance, these souls draw little notice and may appear drab and ungifted, not attractive in any way. Their unremarkable status in the world is consistent with the absence of any striking outward impression. But God has a different gaze on them, which is sometimes evident only well into their lives when his private designs begin to show themselves more strongly. In that sense, these souls can be like the late blooming plants only beautiful at summer's end. But until that time, a loneliness generally accompanies their long journey into serious graces. They usually meet loneliness early in life, and it never leaves them. But it does not harm them. At some point, they learn to retreat to an inner sanctuary of companionship with God in prayer. That he invites them to this discovery is a singular grace; otherwise their lives might suffer unfruitfully. Although hidden from outside eyes for the most part, these souls may be encountered more often than we think. They can be seen at silent hours in the dim shadows and corners of city churches, on bent knees before tabernacles, or settled in a pew with a rosary, seeking the one companion who seems to recognize their singular attentions even as the words they repeat would be tiresome to merely human ears.

~

After a while, God's purpose in keeping such souls in their hidden obscurity may come to light. In all their need and hunger for God over many years, they never realize that their relations with God might change dramatically all at once. Then, later in life, he begins to burn their desires with a different flame. In some of these lives, a desire for God surprising in its intensity invades their prayer late in life in a new manner. A different awareness seems to awaken, and initially they may ignore or even renounce the whispered possibility. They do not realize they have been chosen for a special offering of themselves, but then they begin to sense this truth. It is ordinarily at that time that God takes them to a location in life, as it were, near the nailed feet of Jesus on the cross. Sometimes it is through grave illness or injury, or perhaps by a loss of a rare friendship they might have known. And they do not draw back or close their eyes to this invitation. They accept, despite the pain and perhaps a deeper experience of aloneness. In fact, their whole life has prepared them for this hour of turning completely to God. Without much trouble, they seem to welcome their place at the cross like a child left out of games at the playground who finally finds the friend long desired. And sometimes, without any drama or notice, they become the best of friends with Jesus Christ crucified and his Passion.

～

"What did not lie in *my* plan lay in *God's* plans. And the more often such things happen to me the more lively becomes in me the conviction of my faith that—from God's point of view—nothing is *accidental*, that my entire life, even in the most minute details, was pre-designed in the plans of divine providence and is thus for the all-seeing eye of God a perfect coherence of meaning. Once I begin to realize this, my heart rejoices in anticipation of the light of glory in whose sheen this coherence of meaning will be fully unveiled to me" (Saint Edith Stein, *Essential Writings*).

～

And what unknown hour of surrender has not yet reached out from the shadows of an undramatic life to become the great test of our desire to give ourselves fully to God's love? For many people, this hour may await the soul in later years when the tragic possibilities typically have their day. Many do not realize that their entire life may be rehearsing quietly for the testing of a single hour. Nothing earlier in life may seem to hint at it, and yet it is already in preparation in God's plan. We walk slowly through life in the direction of a time of trial meant to draw out from us the great surrender of our life to God. The death of a spouse when marriage has been a deep bond for decades is a notable example. Grave illness is another, even more when it torments someone we love. At the terrible hour of loss or crushing pain, we are ordinarily not inclined to a great act of surrender to God. Instead, a resistance toward the will of God may be felt strongly for a time. Yet if we have been prayerful in life, this surrender of ourselves beckons gently to our spirit. The prospect of a deep surrender to God may not attract at first, and yet if we enter into a true offering to him, the surrender opens us to the divine presence in a new manner. It is as though an unexpected strong breeze swept into a room and lifted a curtain from a window, and we suddenly can see outside to the stark seriousness of life. Perhaps it is only after an irrecoverable loss that we confront the fragility of everything in life known in love. At that hour, the eventual passing of things is all too evident. If we are fortunate, we will hear eternity calling out to us in that same hour and honor that greeting as a truth beyond our comprehension.

～

If we continue to make this deeper surrender daily before the quiet of a tabernacle, casting a personal loss into the hands of God, offering what will not be returned, but offering it by our choice as a gift given over and over again, the effect is consequential. A threshold is eventually crossed in the renunciation of ourselves that accompanies such an act. The experience of loss becomes the catalyst to a discovery, namely, the attraction our soul has for God when we offer an absolute and full Yes to his will in the time of pain. A tragic loss may cut to the core of a soul. But the offering turns mysteriously into a new realization: that what has been lost has acquired a reverential quality, almost a sense of privilege, uniquely ours to offer. The loss is an event in time, but the offering of it never finishes because it can be renewed again each day. A desire intensifies to offer a more and more complete Yes to what God has chosen. It can become an open

path into the heart of God. It is not unusual, perhaps, that God blesses this gift with great kindness.

⁓

After some time in the long journey of prayer, contemplatives perhaps do not expect so much from
God. It is not that they lack desire. When truly
poor, as they always are, they have little passion
but for God. What they seem to lose over time
is not a passion for God, but the impulse to seek
signs of favor from God. They have learned in a
quite personal manner that he will not grant them
these signs of being favored. Slowly over time, in
a kind of wordless instruction not understood at
first, God crushes in them the desire to receive a
return for their efforts. He refuses the yearning that
burns in a corner of their soul to know they are special to him or favored. At some point, they come
to realize that the identity they have been bringing to prayer, with its disguised traces of egotism,
must be renounced, thrown away as an item of
spiritual interest. They accept finally that every ag-
grandizement of self, especially the subtlest, is an
enemy of prayer. The desire for receiving a reward
of any sort contradicts the necessity of making a
complete surrender to God, of holding nothing in
reserve, of keeping nothing postponed to a later
day. In some cases, it is after years in pursuit of

God that they embrace this essential task of prayer to seek always a purer offering. They cross a threshold as contemplatives when they want nothing any longer for themselves in prayer but to give all for God and for souls. It is only then, perhaps, that prayer's deeper mystery becomes almost a natural home for them.

~

Sometimes with certain souls of greater poverty, God seems to give nothing less than himself. He does not waste time on minor satisfactions. Cloisters and monasteries are a natural habitat for such contemplative souls, but they are hardly confined to a presence behind enclosed walls. A kind of unnamed fraternal order of vagabond contemplatives lives also in the world. These souls have in common that they never find anything in their lives superior to seeking God. God for them is not a curiosity or partial interest, and seeking him is not something taken at a leisurely pace. These souls are impetuous in their desire for God, intense in yearning, yet they seem to receive little return for their passion. If God is close to them, he does not show it by inward signs enjoyed within the soul. Rather, he inflicts an emptiness and aloneness upon them that deepens during life and yet seems to draw them to a more intense desire for himself. In prayer, his divine eyes seem never to pierce their blindness, even when they are most sure of his gaze in the dark hour. For a lifetime, these souls may receive nothing they can call a special gift from God, no tribute to being favored in the eyes of God. And yet they have a mysterious certainty that his presence accompanies and feeds them continually. They endure their prolonged aloneness but do not doubt he is always near. The conviction of his presence is steady and never leaves them. This certitude, even in the darkest hours, is not questioned and is perhaps the true favor they are receiving all along from God.

~

As these souls persevere in prayer, a transformation hidden from their awareness occurs. Confounded in their desire for God, they learn to live with spiritual frustration as a customary state of soul. Chronic dissatisfaction becomes a pure, unhindered path to God. These souls over time seem to adjust to inner emptiness simply by taking little notice of it. They come to experience their inner poverty as ordinary, not something to correct or overcome. To them no other interior life seems possible. Yet, all the while, as they go to prayer and continue to give themselves outside prayer, a spiritual flame within their soul burns secretly with growing intensity. Over time that flame purifies their desire for God until it becomes a steady, quiet yearning never far from their thought. This constant desire for God, while remaining poor before God, becomes their road to God. It is the path walked often by the anonymous saints, of which there are more than a few. This type of life poses trials of spiritual frustration, but once it is understood in its closeness to God, the temptation to disdain or disparage it ceases. Finally embraced as a true sacrificial vocation, and as one's personal path to a great love for God, the poverty can be accepted and serenely offered. Sustenance of soul then takes place in many hidden ways, in the unseen depths of the soul where the poverty itself assuages hunger and the deprivation strangely becomes a form of satiety. The poverty carries the soul to the heart of God himself. Somehow these souls come to know that the poorest depths of their lives conceal an intimacy with God, and they do not want their lives to be otherwise.

~

When Our Lord gives any special gift of himself, it seems often to surprise the contemplative souls who are truly poor. For ordinarily they do not expect gifts from God and have abandoned a desire for them. Signs of regard from God do not draw their longing and expectation, and they do not look for special gifts for themselves in turning to God. Over time, by a certain training in purification, they have become naked and empty in seeking God, as though by holy negligence they have acquired an indifference toward their own satisfaction. An inner passion for God has burned the shards and stubble of lesser longings. When they are really poor, little desire remains in them but for God himself and the good of others. And on a day when Our Lord makes himself more directly known to their interior heart, they are not prepared, they do not anticipate the surprise. They are more accustomed to shadows and the dry interior climate and almost prefer these conditions as their home and resting place for prayer. And yet Our Lord always seems to visit these souls eventually, at times after lengthy intervals, perhaps to remind them of a greater gift that still awaits them. And when he does come, he seems to love these souls of poverty with, indeed, a special regard, communicating his presence in a silent way that cannot be doubted or resisted. In those hours, they have only to glance at a tabernacle and the exalted truth is starkly alive and present in the silence.

∼

Ordinarily, with souls very poor and contemplative, there is no particular request for God to answer. These souls have long abandoned an inclination to petition for themselves. Rather than responding to a request that is not present, God simply gives himself, a gift that exceeds to an extreme any other favor that might come from God. And in giving himself, he comes mostly in the garb of a silent beggar who asks for nothing but an exchange to take place in which a reversal of position occurs. All he seems to want as a beggar is the silent gaze of a longing for himself that will make the soul become a poor beggar, too. No fine words are necessary, no release of exaltation; silent desire replaces words as the preferred language. A yearning for God refined in poverty has taught these contemplative souls the exquisite value of this silent language. They know by experience an understanding without speech when they are in his presence. The gift Our Lord makes of himself in this poverty confirms the useless superfluity of speech. Even brief words of beauty would interfere and cannot compare with the silence of the heart's longing. When his divine presence is near, the soul's desire unites secretly with a presence that communicates to it the silent desire of another. This presence always hides a greater truth that the silence itself cannot enclose or contain or sufficiently honor.

10

Conversion to a Love for Prayer

The fear of prayer: is it fear of illusion, or fear of truth? Fear of psychological complications, or fear of God? And is it not perhaps at the same time fear of finding one's self and fear of losing one's self?

> —Henri de Lubac, S.J.,
> *Paradoxes of Faith*

For many of our contemporaries, religion has been reduced to an experience, one among others, occasionally powerful, but not sufficiently so to draw the rest of their existence into its orbit.

> —Louis Dupré,
> *Religious Mystery*

What happens is that a person thinks so often and so habitually about God in conventional terms that this great reality, which is the sole reality, becomes attenuated behind a screen of phrases that have been learned by rote.

> —Julien Green (in De Lubac,
> *The Discovery of God*)

Conversion in the life of prayer can entail various pos-
sibilities. What may be surprising is that there are souls
meant in God's plan for a serious life of prayer who do
not yet realize this truth in their lives. They require some
experience of a shaking up, a spiritual tumult of sorts, to
bring them to the realization. Otherwise, they risk miss-
ing in life a most serious grace they have been given by
God and frustrating a deeper longing within their soul.
For some people, this deeper awareness may come after
years of an indifferent or routine approach to prayer. In-
deed, the discovery of prayer often seems to require that life
has been lived for a time without a great need for God.
But then the hour comes, and we may begin to sense the
beauty and attraction of silent time in front of a tabernacle
or monstrance. In fact, this phenomenon of souls releasing
themselves from barriers of resistance to prayer and enter-
ing into its adventure is not uncommon today. It is taking
place among many priests, religious, and laity in signifi-
cant numbers, and it is a sign of the God's presence in the
Church in a special manner. "It is unbelievable what a
person of prayer can achieve if he would but close the doors
behind him" (Søren Kierkegaard, Provocations).

Our soul is laid bare in the hour of silence and
solitude. At least that can be our hope, for it is
not always true. Solitude can just as easily deceive
and unbalance our soul when the hungers of a restless imagination take hold and inhabit our mind.
Without some mental discipline of interior silence

in our hours alone, the enchantments of illusion can be hard to resist. In one form or another, the private comforts of unreality are ever ready to reclaim squatter's rights within our soul. For that reason, mental austerity when we are alone is a serious need if we are to live a deeper interior spirituality in truth. By that is meant a deliberate control of the mind's tendency to leap about in needless curiosity, a refusal to drift in reverie, to wander aimlessly into the dusty corners of our mind. Unfortunately, we may find ourselves at times quite captivated by an inner world of our own making. But the habit surely does harm to prayer. Every form of indulgent mental escape is a turning away from the presence of God hiding in the current hour, whether we are in prayer or not. We ignore the sacred presence of God to our own detriment of soul. Silent attentiveness to immediate realities before our eyes—the uniqueness of faces, the beauty of natural scenery, a crucifix on a wall—can be a preliminary way to counter the ill effects of an undisciplined mind. An observant eye taking careful notice of real things involves a concerted exercise of mind as much as of vision. This steady effort of attention is incompatible with a drifting of the mind in impulsive directions. The spiritual fruit of attentiveness may come quickly in a greater sensitivity toward interior promptings from God and in a greater respect for Our Lord in the silence

212 Contemplative Enigmas

of his near presence, without which no deeper interior spirituality can flourish at all.

~

Many people after a time approach prayer as a duty that must be performed even with distaste or reluctance. A sense of obligation drives the practice. Unfortunately, we do not consider the easy collapse of prayer that can take place when we think of prayer only as obligation. The refusal to pray is only a short step away from looking at prayer as a burden. Even more pertinently, we do not like to acknowledge what it really means to excuse our disinclination to prayer. The distaste for giving time to prayer is actually to humiliate Our Lord, but we do not perceive this. An insight from human friendship can perhaps make the point. If someone we thought to be a very good friend begins to avoid contact with us, to cut short our conversations, to leave calls and messages unanswered, we suffer to some extent. The avoidance of contact will cause pain when there is nothing to explain it. In much the same manner, prayer depends on a realization that the human heart of Jesus Christ experiences emotions we cannot fathom. It is a fully human heart even now in heaven and therefore perhaps vulnerable in some mysterious manner to being wounded by our indifference to prayer. We

do not realize that our neglect of prayer, our unconcern for relations with him, may be a way in
which he suffers for the friendship he has chosen.
The human heart cold to prayer, especially in receiving the Eucharist, may pierce the heart of Jesus
Christ with repeated wounds.

⁓

"The true problem of our times is the 'crisis of
God,' the absence of God, disguised by empty religiosity" (Joseph Ratzinger, Conference of the
New Evangelization). Fidelity in spiritual life and
in prayer can easily become an abstract notion,
forced and imposed by habit, stripped of passion
and interior engagement. After a while, the passionless condition is not noticed because it seems
normal. But if fidelity is only external commitment, nothing more, it arrives eventually at a state
of self-contradiction. The things of the spirit require interior dedication and some passion or they
die from lack of sustenance. A repugnance will
grow, hardly recognized, and a sense of the façade
and pretense in spiritual exercises will take over
until it spills over and makes itself felt. What had
been suppressed pain at going through the motions
in prayer shifts one day to a terrible distance from
God. The living presence has disappeared to some
degree and cannot be found. The words of prayer

have begun to sound like echoes in a dark tunnel. With no change taking place, the frustration intensifies and demands a response. Yet many people simply numb themselves to such empty religiosity and take no steps to remedy it.

~

It would seem that indifference to spiritual pursuit does take place for extended periods in many lives meant for close relations with God. There may be long years in which an internal emptiness and a disinterest in God are accepted as an ordinary fact even in the life of prayer. And perhaps many souls prolong this condition by almost stoically assuming that prayer is primarily a matter of duty, not of delight. For them, prayer is a task to complete, a burden shouldered with other obligations, rather than a pursuit of love, a search for someone real and actual and present. There is customarily in such lives no longing for the hour of prayer. They are not inclined to acknowledge their spiritual frustration as a failure of love as long as the duty of prayer continues to be observed. Nonetheless, the reality of emptiness is evident and perhaps occasionally acknowledged. Regularity in prayers may deceive for a time as a sign of fidelity, but no one believes this for very long. In truth, even a steady "faithfulness" in prayer can be a poor cover for the absence of personal relations with God. The truth cannot be concealed forever. The eyes of the soul open sooner or later to its own frustration. What we do with that recognition depends on how serious we are about love. At times, the recognition of little love in prayer leads a soul only to a more stubborn stoicism in prayer. Other times, it awakens in a person a growing dissatisfaction and a demand to encounter God in some real manner. And then there is hope that a soul will realize its true invitation in the life of prayer.

For a soul that has become passionless in prayer, the hour of conversion may catch it off-guard. Nothing prior may give any hint or warning. Until that point in time, the routines of a dull piety may carry on steadily, uninterruptedly, but usually in a stiff, mechanical fashion. External religiosity is observed, prayers are said, but all this is done superficially, with no deeper attention or desire. The recitation of daily prayers has come to resemble Ezekiel's dry bones rattling on a desert plain. This manner of praying without heart has consequences, like a body once athletic now in corpulent decline. The neglect of focus and passion leads predictably to negligence in other areas of life. But then, as some souls testify, a remarkable thing may occur,

one of those unexpected gifts quietly granted by
God, perhaps because the regularity of prayer itself
has never been abandoned. A grace may enter the
setting of prayer, a grace not understood at first.
Discomfort in prayer and restless agitation are initial symptoms, a dissatisfaction felt precisely when
praying. The veneer of superficiality in one's prayer
begins to trouble and vex the heart. The realization
sets in of little happening in religious exercises but
a kind of forced fidelity to a commitment. Soon a
sharp distaste begins to attach itself to the words
rushing past mindlessly and cut off from any deeper
meaning. A need is felt to slow down and find a
sacred tone, a new way of speaking that might re-
store some sacredness to the language of prayer.

~

It may all happen then by surprise, without preparation. Unnoticed, in some small manner, a light
arrives in prayer one day, perhaps while praying
a psalm from the breviary, and suddenly a voice
seems to cry out "stop, wait, be still, do not move."
A need is felt to go back and repeat the same phrase
differently, to explore its sacredness, and to do so
immediately. It can happen on a day when we anticipate nothing from the customary prayers but
the dull, uncomprehending completion of a task.
Unexpectedly, a verse lights up and shines on the

mind, drawing attention—"What else have I in heaven but you? Apart from you I want nothing on earth" (Ps 73:25). Suddenly the words are piercing in their impact, like a slap to the face, almost violent in their insistence that they be repeated. Lifted up anew by a voice aware of their sacredness, they sound very different, spoken now before the very presence of Our Lord. A need may be felt to ponder certain phrases with the anxious thought that their deeper significance has not been fully penetrated. Possibly a loathing is felt at the coldness and indifference with which these same sacred words have been glossed over so many times. A revulsion at all the hours of careless, callous prayer in the past bursts like an infected wound. The thought occurs that so very little has taken hold within the soul in so many hours of prayer. And in that halting silence, perhaps the question is again heard. "What else have I but you?" The feeling expressed in these words can be enough to reverse a life of prayer, bringing a new personal engagement. "Nothing but you, Lord, are important, nothing else do I desire."

～

The aftereffect of such an hour may be notable. The need to leap in sacred words toward God resonates, as it were, in a newly mined portion of soul. The realization can be a true sense of reprieve for the soul. A life perhaps can change in an hour in which a few words of a psalm spoken before the face of God pierce the soul with their full magnitude. Truth comes into sight with a return to a proper respect for prayer. In another sense, it is not a return at all, but an entirely new experience of God in prayer. We cannot pray in the same way once we realize that God is listening at the depth of our soul to the words on our lips. That day it is as though a locked door has opened, with a wind blowing through the open passage. The hour lifts the mask on the emptiness of religious practices that are directed, not to God, but merely to satisfying a human need. It brings as well an insight of more intense faith. The waste and futility of pursuing in life anything less than God himself becomes a lucid and undeniable truth. The conviction that God must be sought passionately, that at all cost he must be encountered, is painfully evident. Nothing else in life can rival or compete with this urgent task.

~

Although we can assume that God certainly wants closer relations with our soul, he may not be inclined to perform miracles for this end. He expects us to seek him in a manner that shows some passion on our part. One practical truth of spirituality seems clear. Only those who at some point in their lives make a passionate choice for God becomes true friends of God. We have to want his deep friendship. This understanding does not deny that God initiates and draws desire to himself in a soul. But closer relations with him demand a choice on our part if we are to discover what is already present in grace. Perhaps the essential heart of that choice is to see what we are willing to sacrifice from our lives for the sake of pursuing Our Lord more intensely in prayer. A passion for God, like other passions in life, requires some degree of dedicated love to prayer, not as an obsession, but as a demand that cannot be denied. Most of all, we have to hunger for being with him in his silent presence in the Eucharist. On many days, we have to accept that "other matters" are secondary to our desire to be with him in a Mass or in the presence of a tabernacle. We must find after a while that we cannot release ourselves from this need to be with *him* in prayer. Then we become even stubborn in our desire to find opportunities for prayer. Perhaps in looking back on our life, it will all seem an inexplicable development after our previous nonchalance and indifference to God. But it is not surprising given a serious choice at some point for Our Lord. The desire to pursue him marks our life thereafter. We can expect that this same desire will be permanent once we have surrendered to it.

~

A sign that a deeper impulse for prayer has awakened in us may be the thought that our preoccupation with God, if it continues in this manner, might make us unfit for normal life in this world. There can be a fear of going too far with God, of taking too great a risk; yet at the same time an unwillingness to pull back. The need felt for God may seem to be getting out of hand, interfering with life, taking up too much interest and time. We may find ourselves, for instance, desiring to visit the quiet of churches rather than indulging former diversions. Soon, we think, a line may be crossed in which God cannot be held at bay. At this point, with these thoughts, we have already passed a barrier without knowing it. We are not thinking about God in a detached manner. He has already become a companion, inciting us to give more of ourselves. In all likelihood we are approaching an hour of choice—to take up the adventure of a serious pursuit after God that may change our life forever or to turn back as though influenced only by a passing dream. The choice is stark: the chance for a deeper experience of God or a life thrown back on common human satisfactions. Many souls seem to sense at some time in life this invitation to seek God as the ultimate quest in life. It is a true crossroad for the soul. Either God will be sought or else he will fade in interest, and then at best a shallow religiosity awaits a life. What is striking, perhaps, is the freedom felt at that juncture of life. Nothing is forced upon us, nothing is so compelling or insistent that we cannot refuse. All is simply an invitation, and we have to choose for ourselves. And every soul that eventually becomes contemplative at some point faces this crossroad and choice.

~

Perhaps an intuitive recognition that unknown sacrifices await our lives is the reason why we sometimes do not seek a deeper life of prayer. We do not ordinarily realize this connection when we first experience an attraction for prayer. Yet there is no soul who gives itself more deeply to prayer who does not discover at the same time a demand for greater sacrifice and self-denial in life. Indeed, sacrificial opportunities seem to rise up conspicuously the more prayer attracts us. These are definite signs of an essential hunger of the soul to give itself more fully to God. And God is responding to that hunger precisely by giving the soul a chance to offer more in sacrifice. The life of prayer, when it is a dedicated pursuit, is always accompanied by providential invitations to live more sacrificially. It is a confirmation that God wants to draw our soul to a greater depth of love in prayer. We should understand the one sign as pointing to the other.

⁓

There is another sign indicating a passion for God awakening in our soul and a deeper desire for prayer. Many things that until then provided escape and diversion in the daily round of life become suddenly tedious and wearisome. There is little or even no enjoyment or relaxation in them but, rather, a sense of waste and banality. The taste for superficial pleasure empties out and disappears. Perhaps this is a sign of a reconstitution taking place in the soul when we become more serious in prayer. Our soul no longer desires cheap sustenance but seeks a richer fare that can be found only in the interior life. The spiritual realm is beginning to light up as a result of prayer, and the attractive glow is felt. The personal presence of God draws our soul, and we want to taste more. Next to the prospect of an encounter with God's presence, there is no worthy rival, nothing that can compete with this new attraction. We now want only to go forward and find what lies ahead in seeking after God.

⁓

There will be no deeper passion for Our Lord without a restless spirit flaring up at times for no appar-

ent reason. It may be evident in our mind turning
to him even without a prayer, in a thirst for his
presence, in an anxiety about what he may now be
asking from us. This incipient passion for Our Lord
may often burn without our recognition while we
go about everyday matters. But when it flames up
and we notice it, it demands a pause for prayer, a
turning of our heart and mind in his direction. Over
time we may learn to perceive the subtle forms of a
spiritual hunger, hardly noticed at times, the small
desires in a day to surrender ourselves to God. They
must be answered with a quiet act and a brief moment of love, but the more intense the better. The
result over time is a passion that extends beyond a
predictable schedule of prayer alone. A passion for
Our Lord is perhaps confirmed above all in the realization that much more of ourselves can be given
to others that has been withheld until now. If the
repercussion of that thought is a certain agitation
of soul, a disturbance to our routines, a desire to
do more for others, all the better. We have to respond to this prompting in concrete generosities
if a passion for God is take its rightful place at the
center of intensity within our soul.

∼

A person who has never known in life a strong
loyalty in love to another person may be unlikely
to become a soul of great commitment to a high

spiritual ideal. We are always capable of deserting an ideal by losing admiration for it, by letting it fade in importance and replacing it with something new. But Christian belief, like marriage, is not enthusiasm for a beautiful ideal. It is to be seized by an intense attraction for the person of Jesus Christ. At a certain point in faith, we must find ourselves overwhelmed in the real presence of Jesus Christ, an encounter that can most certainly take place in the quiet of a chapel or church while alone before a tabernacle. Only then, perhaps, facing invisibly his actual gaze and countenance, does the power of radical Christian belief begin to exercise a compelling attraction. Personal fidelity to the hard demands of holiness is possible only after some deeper experience with the person of Jesus Christ, usually in the presence of the Eucharist. It is Jesus himself in a real encounter who arouses loyalty and a determination to follow him at all costs. The recognition of a particular religious path chosen by him for our life then follows almost as a natural sequence from this encounter. The sense of a "path" now lying before the soul becomes understood as the way to deeper encounters with him. And the soul wants this earnestly. A return to the initial remark may be pertinent. Without some experience of deeper personal loyalty to another person prior to a serious Christian commitment, it can easily happen that the essential demand of Christianity is identified simply as serving the Church in some capacity of faithfulness. But this is certainly not the same as the absolute gift of oneself to God. The latter is pursued at a much deeper level of personal encounter.

~

The tension between external structures and internal conviction is an ongoing challenge in the spiritual life. Harmony between these two principles must be sought and honored. A commitment to disciplined structures of regularity in our spiritual practices—set times for prayer, daily Mass if possible, the reading of Scripture, the recitation of the Rosary—is an essential need. The choice to maintain disciplined habits of prayer in the pursuit of God is a necessary condition for a serious relationship with God. Without them, a hit-or-miss approach is likely adopted and a soul is unstable in its approach to God. Prayer does not develop into a serious commitment. On the other hand, structure in itself is never enough. Deep internal conviction must animate our pursuit of God. The conviction of the Lord's personal choice of ourselves has to be embraced and deepened over time. Conviction is the fire that inflames the structured regularity with loving animation in our daily life of piety. The realization of God's presence available by means of prayer, the Mass, or Scripture read at a slow, steady pace is invaluable for the spiritual life. There has to be a sense of holy and elevated predictability in a life of prayer and pursuit of God. The predictability is not in the routine of practices, but in the expectation that Our Lord is encountered by means of the set times for prayer. The human person thrives on this sense of expectation with God. The conviction that God is met over and over again can be sufficient to keep a soul steady in choosing a consistent regularity in prayer.

~

The presence of disciplined structure is never a guarantee of deeper spirituality. If our conviction in faith is not deepened, the external aspects of structure may begin to gnaw at the human spirit. Conviction is the internal vitality that imbues structure with value and attraction. Without the enhancement of conviction, the value of structure loosens and may eventually collapse. The tragic breakdown of religious life in numerous congregations in the last decades can be traced in part to the displacement of traditional structures of communal living with a more free-wheeling openness in life-style and commitment. The loss of structure was merely symptomatic, however, of a more essential sapping of conviction. When conviction is superficial and the structures themselves become over time burdens to be endured, a small fissure in the wall can soon bring the whole edifice to the ground. Religious life underwent a tragic crisis in these decades primarily because the life of prayer lost a disciplined commitment. Everything is ready to disintegrate, including doctrinal fidelity, when personal relations with Our Lord are no longer sought in earnest.

~

Certainly, the exercise of faith will at times demand a protective instinct, not as its exclusive function, but to identify spiritual danger and to guard against it. Too often, perhaps, this protective instinct is understood only in terms of a vigilance against doctrinal error. But it involves more than doctrinal considerations and fidelity to Catholic faith. In the life of faith, a sterile practice of prayer devoid of a spiritual passion for God is also a spiritual danger. The instinct to preserve our spiritual life from dullness and routine needs periodic reawakening. Choices that return a hunger for God to our soul are not difficult to adopt, but they must be chosen. They allow us to recover what has been lost by neglect, or they enkindle a desire for God we have not known previously. For example, those working in cities who make it a practice to get inside a church each day quickly discover how real God's closeness can be. In effect, they put oil each day on the flame of a spiritual hunger for God. Faith demands that we stoke the passion for God and keep it stirred. Soon we find that steady practices and commitments give a new quality to prayer itself. It becomes less effort and exertion and much more part of a hungering rhythm in a day. It satisfies an attraction felt within the soul that cannot be ignored or taken for granted.

~

It may be that not all religious people long for an abiding peace from their faith. Some people after years of religious commitment may half wish for the drama of a spiritual storm that would sweep in and shake their lives, overcoming their caution and hesitation before God. They half long for an upheaval of sorts by which the face of God would come clearly into focus for their soul. God at that point would become a certitude too radiant and strong to fade so easily from attention. What was for so long blurred and indistinct would now burn with clarity. All desire in life could converge in the one pursuit of seeking and finding God. Turning to him day and night would dominate their existence, and God himself would close off all escape from his presence. At last a unique place in the divine plan could be embraced unreservedly. But, alas, nothing resembling such an experience occurs. And perhaps it is the unreality of these vague wishes that keeps such souls from crossing an actual threshold to a more personal self-offering of the soul to God. If this is to happen, something as simple as an encounter with Our Lord in the Eucharist may wait for them in the quiet silence of a church while praying before a tabernacle. But they must be ready to return repeatedly to a prayer of self-offering, perhaps for many days and for long hours, never giving up their desire to know God. And he is likely to respond to them, as he always does when a soul is resolute in its longing to know him.

II

Hidden Traits and Obscure Struggles

How shall a man attain to the perfection of Charity if he does not keep himself perpetually in the presence of God, and has not the attention of his whole soul fixed on him and primarily on Jesus Crucified in such a way as to "pass through the wounds of his Humanity into the intimacy of the Divinity"?

> —John of Castel,
>   (in Maritain, *Prayer and Intelligence*)

After receiving communion coldly and without any thought which could move me, there came to me a kind of impetus so strong of love for Our Lord that I did not know what was happening to me. It did not last long, but it left me with the thirst to love him more and more.

> —Saint Maria Maravillas of Jesus
>   (unpublished quotation, Brooklyn Carmel)

Ah, who has the power to heal me? Now, wholly surrender Yourself! Do not send me any more messengers, they cannot tell me what I must hear.

—Saint John of the Cross,
The Spiritual Canticle

Contemplatives are a hidden leaven of spiritual presence in this world. But their concealed quality is accompanied as well by hidden testing and adversities peculiar to their state of soul. Most contemplatives do not "fit" so suitably into the setting in which God plants them. They are like irregular brands, as it were, sometimes unconformed and unconventional in their ways, but more often simply unnoticed. It is the necessity of a deeper dedication to God that a soul is often more alone. These souls have their sufferings, but they also have their integrity and passion. The interior life of a greater desire for God will inevitably cause some friction with the necessity of living in a world not so taken up with God. The contemplative urge to be only all for God requires a realism and a capacity to come down from the mountain for the sake of God's plan and for others, while all the while retaining an intense hidden passion for God. "Love not only loves to pour itself out, it also demands to be received" (Raïssa Maritain, Raïssa's Journal).

Those who grow in a depth of contemplative graces manage in one form or another to counter the spiritual crisis of their own time. But they do so in a way that never repeats the holy lives of past eras. The spiritual crisis of each time in history is unique; likewise, the general tenor of sanctity differs in every era. It is true that sanctity at any time will show endless variations in individual lives. Nonetheless, the holy souls of any age form a kind of spiritual counterpoise, an opposition and counterweight, to the rejection of God in that day and age. In our own time, the spiritual crisis of callous indifference to God demands a sanctity of intense religious witness. For those who do want holiness, it is not sufficient simply to support those who are already convinced believers. Today these are too few in number. Nor is it sufficient simply to maintain personal religious practices. The deep urgency now is to go out boldly in search of souls, to win souls for Christ, souls who have become lost in the empty labyrinths of modern life. We live in a world largely unaware of how deeply it denies and ignores God's presence. Demonic whispers of deception hover in the shadowed minds of many lives essentially indifferent to God, many of whom still on occasion attend church. The actual crisis of contemporary unbelief must be confronted above all with a return to serious prayer as the primary weapon against the ancient enemy of Christ and his Church.

～

There is a need to cross thresholds of more intense interiority in the soul over time. We must cross thresholds of insight in which dim lights give way to sharper penetrations. One aspect of this search for insight involves an awareness of living in transient time, especially in the times of struggle or trial. Deeper contemplative insights are never detached from the soul's rootedness in time. While contemplative life enjoys some taste for eternal truth, the soul itself is never disconnected from a historical moment. For that reason, our insights in prayer must often be immersed in the virtue of hope. Our thoughts at times in prayer lean in the direction of what lies ahead, what is coming, of anticipations. It is the nature of every prayerful insight that the soul is being drawn into a sharper perception of truth. God is entering more deeply into the soul, but precisely then does the soul experience God's immanence in time more acutely. With that gift comes also a deeper penetration into the historical moment of time. The presence of God in the current historical moment is realized in tandem with the presence of God within one's own soul. The entry of God in immanence within his creation is understood to take place in both ways. As a result, we perhaps understand better the spiritual crisis of our time and we face more acutely the demands for sacrificial giving that confront us.

~

Contemplatives have a common trait, namely, that a passion for God animates a great undercurrent within their soul. On a retreat in 1997 that I conducted for the Missionaries of Charity in Jordan for their region of the Middle East, one Philippine sister came to me during those days to ask my opinion about a matter. She was assigned at that time to the congregation's work in Hodeida, Yemen. Her regional superior in the congregation was worried that the dreadful heat of Hodeida, which in summer months hovers oppressively at 115–120 degrees, was going to "melt her away" before too long. In that conversation, the sister expressed to me her strong desire to remain where she was, although of course she would obey if a transfer were ordered. She was sure that it was God's will that she was stationed in these hard circumstances of Yemen. She told me that the life she was living now was what she had hoped for in her novitiate. She had prayed then, she said, for the harsher life of greater sacrifice, a life that would stretch the heart to give without counting costs. She told me how much she had grown in her love for the crucified Christ in her time in Yemen and knew much more now his presence in human suffering while taking care of sickly old men in their home. She had found in this location what she was sure was the answer to her earlier prayer. Love and sacrifice had become united in a clear and undeniable way. I replied that she should speak to her superior as she had spoken to me, allowing her heart to be open and transparent. Then let God decide. He will know what he wants and what is best; no need to be anxious. And as she was leaving the room, I remarked, without any real thought behind the words, "But Sister, you know if you return to Yemen, you could become a martyr, no?" She paused with her head down, then looked up with serious eyes. "Father, for a long time, I have desired that." One year later in the same month, in the first year after Mother Teresa's death, early on a hot July morning, after prayer and Mass and breakfast, she and two other Missionaries of Charity were met by an armed assassin who appeared suddenly out of high grass and shot the three Sisters at close range as they were walking down a sandy road from their convent praying a Rosary together on the way to the compound where until that day they had been caring for 220 indigent old men.

~

"It is yearning that makes the heart deep" (Saint Augustine, in Peter Brown, *Augustine of Hippo*). There can be strong, even profound, desires for God experienced in prayer, but what value do they have if they do not urge us to a more sacrificial life? The most reliable mark of a genuine desire for God is the quick discovery outside prayer of sacrificial opportunities for the sake of others. To give ourselves to God in prayer is to find a door in our heart unlocking and opening to the hearts of other people. The effect is felt outside prayer, even immediately. People we have not been accustomed to notice suddenly draw our sympathy and interest. Unknown strangers, especially the poor, will now provoke a visceral reaction of compassion for their suffering and loneliness. The vulnerable condition of forsaken people is mysteriously felt as a chance to love Our Lord himself. It is a part of the beauty of prayer that a desire for God experienced in the private interiority of our soul should sweep us outside ourselves by means of an altered vision. That this phenomenon that people formerly ignored and avoided would suddenly occupy our attention and desire can only be due to the presence of God in them and in us. The lingering sight of suffering in the faces we have met and that still sears our mind long after an encounter can only be because Our Lord himself was hiding in those souls.

$$\sim$$

Contemplative souls seem to observe differently, especially in their contact with the hidden world of souls. In some souls encountered, for instance, it would seem that an almost "apocalyptic" dimension is present. It can be a possible metaphor for the struggle with darkness that smolders within certain wayward lives, as it burns within history itself. These wayward souls carry within them a spiritual tension they are never able to conquer, which tears as well at the inner heart of history. A persistent ambivalence is never overcome in them. They lean toward God one day, toward the devil the next day. One hour they are full of prayer and pleading for help, the next they are edging near the precipice of collapse and despair. Their unsettled, often self-destructive condition of soul is a mirror of humanity itself as it staggers and reels through history. But these souls are not just unstable and erratic, wavering between salvation and loss. They often seem to possess, too, a prophetic impulse, at least regarding their own lives. They sometimes sense a final denouement awaiting their lives; perhaps history itself, as it were, has the same premonition. These souls are sometimes strangely sensitive to the hints of a last drama approaching. Perhaps mindful of their own death, they are souls who in their later years cling with a peculiar passion to God. The thirst for God has never left them, never abandoned them. The weary strain of their darker inclinations has never quenched their faith. Their grip on the hand of God, even sweating and desperate, has remained an abiding truth. All the poison they have imbibed in their wanderings has never managed to suffocate a panting after God. And this quality of indestructible faith is also perhaps a parallel truth of human history. The human soul's hunger for God, despite all efforts to smother it, will never be extinguished from history.

~

Better to be awkward, silent, dismissed as irrelevant, interpreted wrongly, rather than to adopt a contrived, artificial personality. Many people develop an exterior persona to fit into a social ambiance and meet a social need, but at what cost? Often, perhaps, the active contest that takes place in the arena of egos should be shunned and avoided, if one desires a serious life of prayer. We do not belong to the world, insisted Our Lord. We are without weapons in these settings. Perhaps defeat is inevitable in the open field of battle where the stronger egos defend their exalted importance and protect their superiority. Often there may be no better option for a prayerful person than silence, and this is not just good advice for monastic vocations. Any office setting in the workplace has circumstances where remaining quiet at times may bring an immediate blessing. A retreat into silence is not an uncourageous withdrawal, but often requires exertion and strength. It demands a diminishment of self, a release from egoistic defensiveness, useless as that may be. The silence may be misunderstood by others, taken wrongly, frowned upon. But it may produce the great benefit of the reduction of an externalized self that means nothing in the eyes of God. And this lessening of self is always fruitful in hidden ways. We discover the fruits in becoming less in the eyes of the world when we return later to the silence of prayer.

～

The true contemplative's inclination to silence should not be confused with timidity as a matter of temperament. Natural sensitivity to introspective moods may foster some attraction for the inward life. But this aspect of temperament has no direct link to contemplative life. It is at best an initial factor in being drawn to prayer once a relationship with God is discovered. In itself, however, outside the realm of grace and a lived response to God, a natural attraction for quiet means little for contemplative life. It can prove to be a weakness for contemplative life if it inclines a person to withdrawal from a concern for others. The true contemplative is engaged with *reality*, which invariably means a receptivity and openness to real encounters and real people. At the same time, true contemplatives seem somehow

to develop a sixth sense to step backward when necessary in the midst of people, without calling attention to their silence. This is not a silence of withdrawal, exactly, but a respect for the value at times
of a prudent retreat. And it has good reason, for it
helps one withstand the impulse of egoism ready
to assert itself if given the chance. Nonetheless, the
habit of contemplatives of forsaking the battle of
egos can make them look hopelessly inept. Even
this perception proves beneficial to them. To appear as losers among the strong and powerful; to be
no match when aggressive voices raise their pitch;
to forsake the parry and thrust of argumentative ex-
changes; to seem slow and plodding and unclever
—there can be spiritual advantages for the life with
God in forfeiting one's dignity. The focus of contemplatives is on something more fixed and certain
—the invisible presence accompanying their lives
—than the outcome of competitions soon to pass.

∽

The temptation to think critically of others may be
intermittently strong in contemplative lives despite
the desire for greater love. Saint Teresa of Avila in
her autobiography, for instance, writes of this trial
and of an almost desperate desire to be left alone at
times, free of irritating interruption. Insight into
the flaws and defects of others may at times be

more keenly felt. And if this is not realized and resisted firmly, a person may forsake the charity that fostered spiritual growth to that point. What is happening here that a contemplative soul should undergo this testing in charity? One explanation may be that an inclination for truth has intensified in these souls. This makes their vision often more penetrating, capable of carving through the surface of personalities to the disfigured flaws that reside in all of us. But these same perceptions, if not mortified, can easily end up becoming caricatures of the true complexity in every human nature. The darker interpretation never captures the deeper truth hidden in another soul. A poverty lies concealed in every soul beneath flaws and defects. The contemplative must acknowledge the presence of this poverty and exercise a kind of charitable ignorance toward other lives. A certain blindness and naiveté in human relations can be salutary. A blindness that refuses to look at defects in others is a necessity for contemplative love to grow.

~

Contemplatives are often unknown figures in settings of social familiarity, and this includes communities of religious life. Their interior life conceals a hidden identity that does not rise easily to the surface. Their innate awareness in prayer of being known in depth by God, not externally, but known from within the soul, from an inner source, accentuates the realization that only rarely does another person approach close to the hidden truth concealed in them. This sense of being known by God, in a mysterious manner gazed on by God, has consequences. Contemplatives seem usually to show little need or interest in cultivating the contours and edges of a public personality in order to make it appealing to others. Even less are they protective and guarded toward something within themselves that might be walled-in and impregnable. They know the insubstantial, passing character of all manifestation of interior and exterior personality. In the best cases, they simply live their days in the shadows of self-forgetful obscurity. They are teaching a certain truth about the human person, while not aware of it, for exterior personality cannot be identified with the actual truth of self. These contemplative souls do not fight this discrepancy or seek to resolve it in some manner. There is no need to overcome this discordance, but only the need to live with it.

∼

"The true contemplative is a lover of sobriety and obscurity. He prefers all that is quiet, humble, unassuming. He has no taste for spiritual excitements.

They easily weary him. His inclination is to that which seems to be nothing, which tells him little or nothing, which promises him nothing. Only one who can remain at peace in emptiness, without projects or vanities, without speeches to justify his own apparent uselessness, can be safe from the fatal appeal of those spiritual impulses that move him to assert himself and 'be something' in the eyes of other men. But the contemplative is, of all religious men, the most likely to realize that he is not a saint and least anxious to appear one in the eyes of others. He is, in fact, delivered from subjection to appearances, and cares very little about them. At the same time, since he has neither the inclination nor the need to be a rebel, he does not have to advertise his contempt for appearances. He simply neglects them. They no longer interest him. He is quite content to be considered an idiot, if necessary, and in this he has a long tradition behind him" (Thomas Merton, "The Inner Experience").

~

The contemplative, to some degree, may be an unenthusiastic participant in certain aspects of "institutionalized" religion. At first this sounds incompatible with truly religious souls, but in fact it has nothing to do with the observance of external fidelities, which remain firmly intact in their lives.

A deeper explanation is possible. It is the nature of contemplative life to seek the heart of the supernatural realities, including the sacredness of sacramental truths and the truths of religious settings. External structures of religious practice, if not respected properly in their sacredness, can become spiritless and routine, observed without an intensity of passion, as though designed primarily for a steady consistency of response. Religious ritual, even as it contains and hides the utterly sacred, may often be performed without an effort of serious offering before God. Likewise, the wide assortment of institutional practices in monasteries, for instance, can too often seem reduced to keeping activities simply repetitive and efficient. Contemplatives are by nature often intolerant of progress reports and measurable goals. They recoil at quantifiable standards as a measure for a relationship with God, including the communal relationship of a monastery with its God. To the genuine contemplative, it may all seem stifling, without a passion for God, even at times with a disrespect toward God or a betrayal of sacred gifts. Nonetheless, the true contemplatives seem always to find their corner, their niche, their way of living a hidden offering to God that ignores the external obstacle.

～

The life of prayer, if pursued with some dedication, inevitably produces a more solitary spirit. This has nothing to do with isolating ourselves from human contact. On the contrary, as prayer deepens, we are taken more out of ourselves. Rather than withdrawing into an enclosure inside ourselves, cut off from others, we are thrust by an impulse of charity in the direction of others. We become more sensitive to the unique encounters we are enjoying in the present circumstance. Prayer is always a turn by love beyond self, and this inclination remains as a prayerful person returns to the flurry and mix of human contacts. Nonetheless, every prayerful person experiences a sense of unspoken truths received in silence that cannot be shared. The solitude of a prayerful person is an interior solitude, a lingering effect of prayer on the inner spirit. It is sometimes most intensely felt precisely in company with others. Sometimes, in an encounter alone with another person, there is the taste again, as in earlier prayer, of being alone with God.

～

The "sin" of the contemplative is often located in the dynamic of self-giving—a holding back when a stretching forth should take place. This failure is not mainly in the quiet hours of interior pursuit. It has more often to do with concrete refusals in human relations, actual circumstances calling for a gesture of generous kindness, or perhaps when a form of more cautious prudence would urge a turning away from a need difficult to meet. These moments are tests in the contemplative life in which we must give ourselves away foolishly, without care for self, even when the giving appears absurd or useless. If we do not give, we close in on ourselves, holding on tightly for the moment to our most important possession, namely, ourselves. We halt a deeper movement in freedom that might have been possible. These kinds of refusal are at times the primary "sin" of the contemplative, but they become their suffering, also. These refusals in a certain sense come back to haunt their interior life, depending on the sensitivity of a soul. They must be purified and propitiated like any sin, but in this case, by generosities that extend beyond earlier opportunities. This is why, when a soul is seeking God with some intensity, an aspect of imprudent, foolish love is always present to a degree as a sign of this truth. The later generosities are singed by regret for what passed and can no longer be given, and now these souls extend themselves to greater lengths in love. In the end, it is clear that God provokes the deeper desires in all this.

∿

The experience of more intense faith may incline some souls meant for deeper contemplative life to live more dangerously for a time. An impulse to risk oneself, to be reckless in decisions, can attract and entice. The devil may seek to exploit this inclination. Approaching as an angel of light, he will tempt the soul to presume divine protection despite a rash disregard for self. This may involve a lack of physical caution, a refusal to take ordinary measures of care with health. It may entail imprudent choices, a conviction of immunity from moral harm or error. The third temptation of Jesus in the desert is worth recalling. The challenge of the devil that Jesus should cast himself down from the pinnacle of the temple, trusting that the angels will protect him, is a repeated temptation in particular lives. The devil's intent is entirely destructive in such a temptation. He would like us to perceive only a great courage in embarking upon some hazardous venture. He wants us to interpret our inner assurance of protection as a sign of great faith and a guarantee of God's favor. The result, however, is not always fortuitous. In those who are presumptuous in taking excessive risks, the consequence can be a crushed spirit and body and, sometimes, a humbling, long recovery.

～

Sometimes, as we hold steady to the discipline of prayer, we may find ourselves longing outside the time of prayer for a change in our external circumstances of life. Indeed, it can seem that any change will do. A desire for something new and unfamiliar burrows inside our soul like an animal that gets inside the wall of a house and leaves us no peace. In part, this mild agitation should be ignored, but it is also understandable. The routine of prayer has a way of rousing our interior spirit to a periodic restlessness. And perhaps this restlessness is a protection against stagnancy in our desire for God. But we might also consider that it is really only the external aspect of our life that is affected by this reaction. In going to prayer, we are always engaging ourselves in a new encounter with God. Some element of the unfamiliar rises up in every new hour of prayer. Prayer is always a fresh experience of placing ourselves before the loving gaze of God's eyes. But we have to remind ourselves of this truth, because the same pattern also has the effect of arousing a desire for new experiences simply for the sake of the change. The fact is that prayer is always a preparation for a fresh encounter with God's providential invitation to our sacrificial offerings of a day. We must be alert for this aspect of the unfamiliar that accompanies prayer and not long for change in location, people, or work simply for the sake of change.

~

A common temptation within contemplative life
is to be internally slothful when nothing seems to
arouse spiritual attraction. The dissatisfaction of
not finding God, of clinging to him by raw faith,
can weigh heavily. If for some time there seems to
be no encounter with God's presence, no new discovery in reading Scripture, no sign of divine providence intervening in the day, spiritual pursuit can
seem a weary, unrewarding grind. Repetition and
routine can reduce the spiritual life to a predictable
tedium. Perhaps the sense of monotony is unavoidable, given a daily set of required tasks and exercises. But instead of a determined, dogged pursuit
of God, which is a necessity at times, a soul may
give way to a dulling of desire that is dangerous if
it should continue. The soul can become lethargic
and empty of purpose, no longer seeking to give
itself to God with desire. We can lose interest in
God in a way similar to the loss of love for a person once close to us. Always, there must be an element of personal choice in our spiritual condition.
If we do not seek attraction in what we are doing
in spiritual exercises, our faculty of will receives
no desire to choose very strongly. An absence of
drive for things spiritual will in turn ensue; it does
not take much to undermine the search for God.
Fatigue of soul can trade places with a passion for

God quite swiftly. Perhaps the only answer is taking ourselves to the quiet presence of the tabernacle, forcing ourselves if necessary not to leave Our Lord's company. It is the one remedy that we will find again and again restores our deeper desire for God.

~

"Apart from me you can do nothing" (Jn 15:5). What is Our Lord trying to teach us in these words? The first impression is an incapacity to do anything spiritually fruitful without him. Clearly enough, we have to remain in a union of heart and soul with him if we are to accomplish any enduring good. Nothing lasting and permanent will result from our life's works unless our efforts have their impetus and source within the heart of Jesus Christ. But there may be a significant meaning in these words that is not considered. In remaining deeply rooted in him, seeking to offer ourselves prayerfully to him, we may find ourselves at times confronting a terrible helplessness and inability to aid another soul in grave spiritual danger. Our efforts for a soul, our fervent petitions, do not seem to bring any sign of change. In this case, the words take on a different resonance. For an experience of powerlessness may overwhelm us most acutely in those times we turn to Jesus interceding for a soul. In that case, at a deeper level, these words of

John's Gospel articulate a further truth in what it means never to be apart from Our Lord. For he himself, even as God, knew an incapacity to assist souls who rejected him. "*I can do all things when I am loved,*" Our Lord said in a locution to the cloistered Jerusalem Poor Clare Sister Mary of the Holy Trinity, "*but if I am not loved, I am powerless.*" We may come to know, too, this powerlessness, this pain of being unable to bring to him souls who want no part of Our Lord's love. And in this we share a taste of Our Lord's own Passion.

12

Some Last Thoughts

God is not a spectacle. The contemplation of him is something more secret, veiled and disconcerting. He is only discovered, and then only in a certain degree, in the fidelity of our movement towards him, in a "passover" which brings peace out of suffering and gives riches at the cost of stripping ourselves of everything.

> —Jacques Paliard (in De Lubac, *The Discovery of God*)

There is much to fathom in Christ, for He is like an abundant mine with many recesses of treasures, so that however deep men go they never reach the end or bottom, but rather in every recess find new veins with new riches everywhere.

> —Saint John of the Cross, *The Spiritual Canticle*

If we don't love God, God seems far away; if we love him a great deal, God is close to us. It's very curious: it's not knowledge that gives us God's proximity, it's his love, because God loves us tenderly.

—Marie-Dominique Philippe, O.P.,
Conference in Rome, February 14, 2006

The manner in which God draws some souls to himself cannot be explained. It is known by souls who experience it, but they are at a loss to know why their desire for God holds them in a relentless grip. There seems no obvious reason for this, no explanation that might be sought. It has nothing to do with reward or favor for good behavior. The experience of a love in God for their soul is simply beyond question. They know this love in the silence of prayer, yet it exceeds understanding and analysis. It is real, not brief or intermittent, not only on rare occasions, but as a quiet certitude that remains always with them. Perhaps these souls gave themselves fully to God in an hour of surrender they cannot remember. On a day in the unknown past, they crossed a boundary in their relations with God, and they never turned back. They cannot say when this might have occurred. It is not an event traceable in time to a particular hour, yet it seems certain and indisputable. These souls have come to know that they belong only to God. "Christ's love possesses the utmost tact. It knows how to combine the most intense demands with the most exquisite unobtrusiveness" (Hans Urs von Balthasar, The Grain of Wheat).

An intense longing for God in prayer is inseparable from our heart becoming purer toward all things encountered outside prayer. The longing for God that we experience in prayer makes even the routine matters of a day more sacred in their impact. This effect of serious prayer does not require from us a particular effort. The longing for God in the privacy of prayer does not simply end with the conclusion of prayer. It has repercussions and effects that stretch beyond prayer. The longing of our soul for God lifts the veil, as it were, from the common appearances of reality around us and instills them with attraction. In particular, our encounters with people after prayer may easily draw us toward their unique individuality. We may see in others a vulnerability and attraction that have been quite new and unnoticed until then.

~

To know oneself as known by God is an essential requirement for love in prayer. This knowledge, however, cannot be sought in terms of a concrete understanding. An effort to "know oneself" is not the same thing as the prayerful awareness of knowing oneself as known to God. Seeking exclusively to know oneself by an effort of self-examination is not enough. That may have its importance at other times, at the end of the day, for instance, or when we are preparing for the sacrament of confession. But in the silence of contemplative prayer, the soul seeks only to enter into a simple awareness of remaining under the gaze of God's loving knowledge. That is all that is necessary for love, but it is a great task. Knowing oneself as known by God in the silence of prayer is to realize a layer of unseen depth in the soul where God directs his gaze of love.

∼

We cannot just enter into silent prayer as we would open a door into a familiar room. Everything we do outside of prayer is a preparation and affects an interior need for God that we bring to prayer. Without a search for the presence of God in the routine activities of a day and a longing for him prior to a time of prayer, we will find ourselves outside a door when we come to pray, unable to cross a threshold. Our insufficiency without God must be a truth already well known before we take our knees to prayer. And perhaps that awareness can be enhanced simply by pausing often in a day to turn in a receptive spirit to the presence of God as the hidden companion immediately at our side.

∼

The separation between all varieties of false and genuine spirituality might be noted in the minor detail of the menial physical tasks of our daily life that can be cast off on someone else to take care of. The prayerful person does not look to be waited on, to have subordinates to do his bidding. Surely it was not the habit of saints to have servants to clear the tables and clean the dishes, to wash and fold the clothes. Our Lord's words urging us to serve and not be served would seem at the least to require a spirit of sincere friendship toward anyone in a role of service to us. Our spiritual character is quite exposed in our treatment of the smaller people in contact with our lives, the people who may be doing menial work for us in some form or another. Our kindness and gratitude to them reveal our soul. They confront us with a chance to reverse roles at times and in some creative manner to show ourselves ready to be a servant to the one who serves.

∼

Every self-absorbed mood outside the time of prayer is a precursor to difficulty in silent prayer. Getting caught up in ourselves, in hurt or anger or a brooding resentment or in anxieties and worries, will carry over into the silence of prayer. The jarring distractions that obstruct prayer at such times, no matter what their content, are symptomatic of a prior indulgence in thinking too much of ourselves. Underlying these distractions may be a confused wish to escape from the thought of self. But this release from self does not occur if we have taken ourselves too seriously before coming to prayer. We do not simply leave our egoism aside as though on a coat rack when we go to pray. It must be overcome in the daily regime of humiliation and sacrifice and a willingness to forget ourselves and think first of others. When we are more taken up with the needs of others outside prayer, we have a much better disposition to turn toward God self-forgetfully in prayer.

~

In brief silences during prayer, there can be a sense that God's gaze on our soul is continuous and abiding, that he watches our soul with love even when our own eyes are closed to him. But it seems we can never hold this thought for very long. And it cannot be self-consciously held, or it dissipates as a reality immediately. Nonetheless, we can deepen its impact upon our soul by an effort of gratitude in remembering what God has done for us in life. The evidence of his personal gaze on our life comes more easily with a glance of gratitude. In the present hour, it may be true that his gaze of love is hard to fathom. But we have abundant evidence of his kindness and solicitude from our past experiences. The mere advertence to the fact is often enough to release our heart's love for him.

～

"God is the soul of our soul: that is, the Principle that gives it life. It is *there* that we must seek Him, and it is there we shall find Him 'without end'. That is what the saints did. They kept themselves . . . *before the face of the living God*. And God, thus contemplated by an interior regard, communicated Himself to them and lived in them. . . . It can be so with us, even in our busiest moments. It is not necessary to seek the stillness of a sanctuary. . . . All we need to do is to make an act of faith and love: 'My God, I believe in you, and I love you': a simple movement in the depths of our soul that we call forth from time to time" (Augustín Guillerand, *They Speak by Silences*).

～

Are the silences we confront in our interior prayer a reflection of an incapacity to hear? A failure to listen to a voice that is present but does not draw our recognition? An unwillingness to wait patiently for a word not yet spoken? There are hidden truths that we may overlook and miss that are much closer to our discovery if only we plunge more deeply into the encounter with God's mysterious *silent* presence in prayer. It is a conversion we must pray for and seek continually as we pursue the life of prayer. We may then realize more deeply God's desire that we offer ourselves in a complete immolation for souls.

∼

"Extinguish these miseries, since no one else can stamp them out; and may my eyes behold You, because You are their light, and I would open them to You alone" (Saint John of the Cross, *The Spiritual Canticle*). Souls aware of a discontent within their heart, caught between a partial need for God and a desire for deeper relations with him, are much better off than those who suffer no such internal tension. The tension is preferable to a false peace and in effect notifies our soul that we cannot ignore God and find any deeper happiness in life. It is a sign that God is drawing our soul and that we might yet turn more fully to him. In the meantime, however, as long as this irresolution remains, we cannot really be happy.

∼

Without someone in our lives who knows us deeply, before whom nothing is hidden or disguised, we are liable to ignore the real poverty that resides in our soul. And we may miss, too, the beauty that God has planted in a concealed manner within us. With both these losses, we may not be aware at all of the actual attraction our soul has for God. At the very least, this demands that we have a steady confessor who hears our soul's repetitive ache and cry for God's forgiveness. Indeed, those who do not face an inner need to be known fully, not for the sake of their appealing qualities or achievements, but in their poverty, are likely to forfeit a great privilege of the spiritual life. They will never come to know being loved by God in a deeper portion of the soul, where the nakedness and need of the soul and its unseen beauty are gazed upon by God.

∼

The soul upset with aridity in prayer may be unhappy with the poverty it tastes in this experience of deprivation. Such a soul is bound to suffer frustration in its prayer as long as its nothingness before God is not embraced. This recognition has to take place first, and then perhaps a prolonged aridity in prayer is no longer an intimidating, anxious trial but, rather, perceived as an offering and sacrifice a soul must make to God. Indeed, it is often not enough to hear that love does not depend on feelings. It is necessary to know an additional truth, namely, that love requires a quite personal experience of one's own poverty and need before God.

～

The desire for a sign that God is close, still watching and protective, becomes more urgent at some junctures in life. Every tense hour of uncertainty, in serious sickness or after a job loss, for instance, should become a time spent more on our knees. But if we seek Our Lord in prayer with real passion, this need for the surety of his closeness will be for reasons that have nothing to do with aid in a time of trial. Once we cross a threshold of intimacy with him, we can expect for the rest of our lives an increasing desire to stay near to him in the depth of our interior life. At times we may find we want a sign of solicitude and near presence, while he seems to declare over and over to our soul that we do not need any special sign. We are now his and belong to him in everything, and all that he has is ours. We must live from this deeper layer of assurance that is perhaps best known to blind and simple souls.

～

Religious sentimentality is naturally a hindrance to a deeper life of prayer. As a form of superficial religiosity, it tends to make a feeling of inner peace the goal of spiritual life. It avoids the hard confrontation with personal sinfulness and adopts instead a soft image of a God who asks no questions, makes no objection, who at most frowns temporarily on forbidden conduct. What it wants from God is assurance of his favor, perhaps little else. If a self-examination takes place, the thought returns on cue that one is doing the best one can, and God can ask nothing more. This notion of an undemanding God, tireless in his indulgent love, can become a kind of personal religious doctrine. It can be trusted at least to bestow benefits upon a person's self-esteem. If sought with determination, a confidence in God's perpetual approval may impart some steady tranquility to a soul. But it does so only by the thought of God becoming an exercise of imagination. If there is a commitment to prayer, as there may be to a degree in such lives, it must include hours deaf to Our Lord in his agony asking from the cross how far are we willing to stretch our lives in generous love for him.

∼

There will always be souls who conceive emotional consolation received in prayer as a sign of divine approval and a confirmation of their closeness to God. And these same people often consider a constancy in outward joy a necessary mark of holiness. They take seriously the effort of *feeling* happy and make this a habit in their own lives, that is, to feel the satisfaction of personal joy. Some of the same people, however, tend to avoid souls not so favored, perhaps wary of losing something precious by a contact with those not so happy. They may fear the harm of a contagious illness in getting too close to people who suffer and are not happy. They keep their distance and avoid such lives. There could be a question raised about what God sees in this caution. Not always does a dedication to prayer produce the fruits of charity that we would expect.

∼

"Our annihilation is the most powerful means we have of uniting ourselves to Jesus and of doing good to souls" (Blessed Charles de Foucauld, in Jacques Maritain, *Moral Philosophy*). Am I, in the long course of this life, telling myself a story of which the most appealing elements are fictional creations of what I would like to be in an ideal version of myself? Real spiritual life requires facing hard facts. Conversion can be wrenching; painful sacrifice can seem to bring nothing but fatigue;

problems around us remain unresolved despite prayer. None of the actual living out of a life close to God may support a soul in a feeling of being favored by God. Deeper spirituality, in other words, has little in common with the musings of a romantic imagination. Those inclined to lovely sentiments in their relations with God either persevere in illusions or get disappointed in due time with God. He is a God, not of sentimentality, but of hard and holy truths. And what, we might ask, grants entry into the primary truth that forms a genuine spirituality? An hour in front of a vividly portrayed crucifixion in a quiet side altar of a Catholic church may be sufficient to drive the lesson home.

~

Much better for our soul to accept that the transcendent mystery of God's actions often cannot be explained than to harbor a quiet resentment that they have no reason and make no sense. What he chooses and permits in our lives has unseen repercussions that may not be understood until a later time. "What I am doing you do not know now, but afterward you will understand" (Jn 13:7). We forget perhaps that God's designs never concern us alone. There is always a network of influences that vibrate at the hand of God upon many lives all at once. The intersecting purposes concealed in events touch many lives at the same time and extend far beyond our meager knowledge. We have to learn a discipline of soul not to question what we cannot understand for the moment. Who can say without God's eyes what Our Lord perceives in the vast interweaving of human lives under divine providence. With greater humility, we will accept more easily that on many days we are playing the part of bit players in an immense drama of goodness directed by the hand of Almighty God.

~

God of course speaks in the coincidences found in events: at times dramatically, other times more quietly. There are random encounters with people, for instance, that might be chance or fate except that our life is sometimes deeply affected by them for long periods of time. There are as well on any day small opportunities that suddenly appear for a generous action without a thought of this a minute before. In all this, God is addressing himself to us, and we can miss it. When we do ignore him, it is not the ineffable mystery of God that makes us uncomprehending. We simply do not acknowledge within our heart a voice other than our own, speaking in a silence not like our own, asking us to listen and perceive and to act on his prompting.

~

If the question is raised about what constitutes a true religious experience of God, perhaps we should consult, not books or theologians, but those who cannot live a day without prayer. That might be the nearest child, or it might be a poor man on the street. We need not expect rapt descriptions of God from them. The most genuine experiences of God are often cloaked in ordinary words and concealed within common events. And the person who recounts them is often unaware of any special favor. In most cases, they may assume that their own experience is typical of all such experiences. Saint Padre Pio, when he was granted visions of angels as a child, thought all children received such visions. Then there is the example of a small child busy with her coloring book who, when asked what she was drawing, responded that she was drawing the face of God. When told that no one has ever seen God, she looked surprised and put her drawing hand back to work and replied in a firm tone not to go away if there really was a desire to see the face of God.

~

We might think that doubts about God would diminish the desire to think about him. But for some people, it may be that the more God seems a questionable notion, the more they want to arrive at a conclusion and a certainty about him. They find their inner state of indecision about God a painful tension. Yet perhaps they will only find the answer they seek by relinquishing a mental habit of treating God as a kind of intellectual conundrum. God is not a puzzle to be solved. Their effort of thought is cold and impersonal and has made a real encounter with God next to impossible. Indeed, there is only a single sure way to resolve this uncertainty. The knowledge that God is personal and real and wants a soul to realize this truth happens on the condition we begin to pray in an utterly personal manner, speaking words of the heart to a God who we are certain is listening in that very hour.

$\sim$

What will be the effect on children's openness to God as they increasingly undergo their earliest experience of play in the "virtual realities" of technological diversions? The new model of play for children as an exercise of private fantasy enacted on a screen at the touch of a keyboard—is this going to blunt irreparably the natural hunger of young souls for an invisible God? Staring for long hours at a screen of moving images may be a harbinger of a dull soul unable to pray. Eyes fixated by a screen require no real effort. The act stifles natural curiosity and a spirit of adventure. There is no great need to seek and find with imagination, no provoking of hunger to create and discover what is not present and not yet known. All becomes an operation of easy impulse. The future health of a spiritual life may suffer as a result. The inability to engage invisible realities cannot bode well for a soul. The need to turn in prayer with eyes closed, to direct one's thought and being to an invisible presence, may not be so easily possible. We ought to know before it is too late that the capacity to believe and to pray requires a comfort with silence and an absence of other stimuli. The crisis of our day may soon be a crisis of an inability for prayer felt acutely by the children of the current day.

~

How ready are we to renounce the satisfaction of personal accomplishments if this is required for love for God? Are we able to accept failure and greater poverty if this is God's will? Have we considered the possibility of unknown losses and deprivation that may await our pursuit of God? These questions must be confronted before the greater contemplative challenges are faced. It is a different and deeper question if we are asked later by God whether we are willing to continue on blindly into the darkness that hides and encloses the infinite mystery of God. This question can arrive only after we have become poor in our clinging to the Person of Jesus Christ. But perhaps no one hears that second challenge of a contemplative life unless the earlier questions have been answered with a fundamental spiritual courage.

∽

Everyone without exception has a childlike quality that may coarsen somewhat with the experience of life and will sometimes seem to disappear. On the other hand, surprisingly, there is often an element of goodness retained in souls who have plunged headlong into wrongdoing. This presence of goodness can almost resemble a lingering innocence untouched by the transgressions of a life. Priests certainly see this kind of remarkable resilience of the human soul, which remains at its root capable of burning again with goodness. The presence of absolute loyalty in a man who is finally listened to by a priest, for instance, or the effusive overflow of gratitude when someone receives unexpected kindness—do these responses depend on extraordinary immediate graces from God, or do they testify as well to deep springs in a human person that evil cannot poison?

∽

"Only the person who renounces self-importance, who no longer struggles to defend or assert himself, can be large enough for God's boundless action" (Saint Edith Stein, *Thoughts of Edith Stein*). The peculiar appeal of self-importance that overtakes souls no matter what their condition in life is an indulgence no soul desiring holiness can ignore. The tendency is bound to tempt even the most insignificant lives. The poor, too, succumb at times to asserting their superiority among their companions. This irremediable tendency in humanity to lift ourselves in importance above others is in fact a weakness that leads to our own unhappiness. The aspiring contemplative must face this tendency and conquer it in his own soul. Even more, the longing to be unimportant and unnoticed in the eyes of others must be a cultivated desire on the contemplative path. The desire for hiddenness is a secret to the deeper peace and happiness of contemplatives. They are no longer so vulnerable to the frustrations that accrue from vanities.

~

What is ephemeral in life, passing, fading away, despite an appearance of permanence, demands a steady effort of spiritual perception, for it raises a question. If we allow ourselves to be seduced by a veneer of great significance in passing things, will we not miss what has true importance in this life? The remembrance of an eternal threshold that we must cross one day is bound to diminish an excessive dependence on the fleeting attractions of passing realities. Who in the next life, for example, is honored for worldly achievements? Who will care in heaven how much money was earned in this life? Who continues to be addressed with titles and marks of deferential respect? Will a cardinal of the Catholic Church still be called "your eminence" into eternity? The only worthy pursuit is for greater love and humility, which indeed we will carry with us into the next life. The lightness we experience in stepping back in detachment from passing things is always a gain in perspective. It is a taste of the true vision of the presence of God in the midst of time. "All is fleeting. . . . Who possesses God nothing wants. God alone suffices" (Saint Teresa of Avila, *Poetry*).

~

It is the nature of the sacred that we should feel unfit and unworthy in its presence. We stand apart, separated, due to our sense of distance. Yet in drawing nearer to the sacredness that is God himself, we come to another understanding. The sacred is also a place of vulnerability in God. What is most sacred often hides in the most common appearance, and

precisely in concealment it is vulnerable to disrespect. God himself is vulnerable in this manner. He
leaves himself by his own humble design open to
betrayal, to being ignored, brushed aside, treated
with casual indifference. The sacredness of the Eucharist is the supreme instance of this vulnerability
in God. Yet perhaps we rarely consider how evident this truth is in our own day.

~

Even in a time of spiritual darkness and ecclesial
crisis, the soul immersed in God is not shaken or
deflected. It continues its quest for a complete gift
to God. It perceives the ecclesial crisis with sor-
row and suffering, but it does not stop there; it has
an answer in an intense life of faith and hope and
charity. God's presence does not change, even in
dense shadows. In some contemplative souls, there
is no impulse to protest the collapse in a culture
of religious certitudes and immutable truths. They
stay out of the public fray, not from reluctance
or detachment, but aware of a greater need. God
has taken their inner passion captive, and nothing
can alter this most certain truth. Prayer and sacrificial offering are their recourse. They trust in
these alone. They know with certitude that these
bear eternal fruits in the lives of souls, and that is

ultimately what matters. All else is passing trial and tribulation and will not perdure.

~

Near the muddy banks of a surging African river in the season of the rains were a series of small whirlpools resisting the rush of the current. The force of the river seemed not to touch them. They remained apart and separate, and the river did not hinder the twisting pockets of water. These small cachets of spinning water had an equilibrium of their own, almost a privacy of their own. All the while, the river pressed on like a magnet pulling brown liquid steel. The flow of the river was all strength and power and turbulence, the water on the surface colliding at times and bouncing into the air. At one point, a child's small sandal moving fast in the current entered one of the whirlpools near the bank of the river, swept around in a circle, then plunged and was swallowed. But the disappearance was short; a moment later it was cast forth with a quick leap, unleashed back into the swift current. And soon that sandal was beyond sight, gone forever.

Bibliography

Augustine, Saint. *The Saint Augustine LifeGuide: Words to Live by from the Great Christian Saint.* Translated by Silvano Borruso. South Bend, Ind.: Saint Augustine's Press, 2006.

Balthasar, Hans Urs von. *The Grain of Wheat: Aphorisms.* Translated by Erasmo Leiva-Merikakis. San Francisco: Ignatius Press, 1995.

———. *The Way of the Cross.* Translated by Libreria Editrice Vaticana (Via Crucis, 1988). Boston: Saint Paul Books and Media, 1990.

Barré, Jean-Luc. *Jacques and Raïssa Maritain: Beggars for Heaven.* Translated by Bernard E. Doering. South Bend, Ind.: University of Notre Dame Press, 2005.

Brown, Peter. *Augustine of Hippo.* 2nd edition, revised with new epilogue. Berkeley, Calif.: University of California Press, 2000.

Chadwick, Henry. *Augustine.* Oxford: Oxford University Press, 1986.

Congar, Yves. *I Believe in the Holy Spirit*, vols. 1–3. Translated by David Smith. New York: Crossroad, 1997.

Dupré, Louis. *Religious Mystery and Rational Reflection: Excursions in the Phenomenology and Philosophy of Religion*. Grand Rapids, Mich.: Eerdmans, 1998.

Evagrius Ponticus. *The Praktikos and Chapters on Prayer*. Translated by John Eudes Bamberger. Kalamazoo, Mich.: Cistercian, 1981.

Faustina Kowalska, Saint. *Diary: Divine Mercy in My Soul*. Translated by Archbishop George Pearce, S.M. et al. 3rd edition. Stockbridge, Mass.: Marians of the Immaculate Conception, 1996.

Foucauld, Charles de. *The Spiritual Autobiography of Charles de Foucauld*. Translated by J. Holland Smith and edited and annotated by Jean-François Six. New York: Kenedy & Sons, 1964.

Gaál, Emery de. *The Theology of Pope Benedict XVI: The Christocentric Shift*. New York: Palgrave Macmillan, 2010.

Guillerand, Augustín. *They Speak by Silences*, by a Carthusian. Translated by a Monk of Parkminster. 1955; Leominster: Gracewing, 2006.

Herbstrith, Waltraud. *Edith Stein: A Biography*. Translated by Father Bernard Bonowitz, O.C.S.O.

2nd English ed. San Francisco: Ignatius Press, 1992.

John of the Cross, Saint. *The Spiritual Canticle, The Ascent of Mount Carmel, The Spiritual Canticle, The Letters.* In *The Collected Works of St John of the Cross*, translated by Kieran Kavanaugh, O.C.D., and Otilio Rodriguez, O.C.D. Revised ed. 1991, Washington, D.C.: ICS Publications, Institute of Carmelite Studies, 2017.

Johnston, William. *The Mysticism of the Cloud of Unknowing: A Modern Interpretation.* St. Meinrad, Ind.: Abbey Press, 1975.

Keating, Thomas. *The Thomas Keating Reader: Selected Writings from the Contemplative Outreach Newsletter.* Herndon, Va.: Lantern Books, 2012.

Kierkegaard, Søren. *Provocations: Spiritual Writings of Kierkegaard.* Compiled and edited by Charles E. Moore. Farmington, Penn.: Plough Publishing House, 1999.

Labat, Elisabeth-Paule, O.S.B. *The Presence of God.* Translated by David Smith. New York: Paulist Press, 1980.

Lane, Belden C. *The Solace of Fierce Landscapes: Exploring Desert and Mountain Spirituality.* New York: Oxford University Press, 1998.

Leiva-Merikakis, Erasmo. *Fire of Mercy, Heart of the Word.* Vol. 2 of *Meditations on the Gospel according to Saint Matthew*. San Francisco: Ignatius Press, 2003.

Liturgy of the Hours, The. Vol. 4. New York: Catholic Book Publishing, 1975.

Lubac, Henri de, S.J. *The Discovery of God*. Translated by Alexander Dru and footnotes translated by Mark Sebanc and Cassian Fulsome, O.S.B. Grand Rapids, Mich.: Eerdmans, 1996.

———. *Paradoxes of Faith*. Translated by Paule Simon and Sadie Kreilkamp. San Francisco: Ignatius Press, 1987.

Maritain, Jacques. *The Degrees of Knowledge*. Translated under the supervision of Gerald B. Phelan. New York: Charles Scribner's Sons, 1959.

———. *Moral Philosophy: An Historical and Critical Survey of the Great Systems*. Translated by Marshall Suther et al. New York: Scribner, 1964.

———. and Raïssa. *Prayer and Intelligence*. Translated by Algar Thorold. New York: Sheed & Ward, 1943.

Maritain, Raïssa. *Raissa's Journal: presented by Jacques Maritain*. Translated by Magi Books, Inc. Albany, N.Y.: Magi Books, 1974.

Mary of the Holy Trinity, Sister. *The Spiritual Legacy of Sister Mary of the Holy Trinity: Poor Clare of Jerusalem (1901–1942)*. Edited by Silvère Van

Den Broeck, O.F.M. Rockford, Ill.: TAN Books, 1981.

Merton, Thomas. "The Inner Experience: Some Dangers in Contemplation (VI)", *Cistercian Studies* 19.2 (1984): 139–50, at 141.

Newman, John Henry. *An Essay in Aid of a Grammar of Assent.* Edited by Paul A. Böer, Sr. Veritatis Splendor, 2016.

Ondaatje, Michael. *The English Patient.* New York: Vintage Books, 1992.

Pieper, Josef. *A Brief Reader on the Virtues of the Human Heart.* Translated by Paul C. Duggan. San Francisco: Ignatius Press, 1991.

Posselt, Teresia Renata O.C.D., *Edith Stein: The Life of a Philosopher and Carmelite.* Washington, D.C.: ICS Publications, 2005.

Ratzinger, Joseph. *Behold the Pierced One: An Approach to a Spiritual Christology.* Translated by Graham Harrison. San Francisco: Ignatius Press, 1986.

———. Conference on the Theme of the New Evangelization at the Jubilee of Catechists and Religion Teachers, December 10, 2000.

———. *Introduction to Christianity.* Translated by J. R. Foster. New York: Herder and Herder, 1970.

Saint-Exupéry, Antoine de. Citadelle, in Œuvres (Paris: Gallimard, Bibliothèque de la Pléiade, 1959). Translated and quoted by Erasmo Leiva-Merikakis in *Fire of Mercy, Heart of the Word.* Vol. 2 of *Meditations on the Gospel according to Saint Matthew.* San Francisco: Ignatius Press, 2003.

Stein, Edith (Sister Benedicta of the Cross), Saint. *Edith Stein: Essential Writings.* Edited by John Sullivan, O.C.D. Maryknoll, N.Y.: Orbis Books, 2002.

——. *Thoughts of Edith Stein.* Eugene, Ore.: Carmel of Maria Regina, undated.

Teresa of Avila, Saint. *Teresa of Ávila: Ecstasy and Common Sense.* Edited by Tessa Bielecki. Boston, Mass.: Shambhala Publications, 1996.

——. *The Book of Her Life.* In vol. 1 of *The Collected Works of St. Teresa of Avila,* translated by Kieran Kavanaugh, O.C.D., and Otilio Rodriguez, O.C.D. Washington, D.C.: ICS Publications, Institute of Carmelite Studies, 1976.

——. *The Interior Castle.* In vol. 2 of *The Collected Works of St. Teresa of Avila,* translated by Kieran Kavanaugh, O.C.D., and Otilio Rodriguez, O.C.D. Washington, D.C.: ICS Publications, Institute of Carmelite Studies, 1980.

——. *Poetry.* In vol. 3 of *The Collected Works of St. Teresa of Avila,* translated by Kieran Kavanaugh, O.C.D., and Otilio Rodriguez, O.C.D. Washington, D.C.: ICS Publications, Institute of Carmelite Studies, 1985.

———. Vol. 4 of *Sermon in a Sentence: A Treasure of Quotations on the Spiritual Life*, selected and arranged by John P. McClernon. San Francisco: Ignatius Press, 2002.

Teresa, Mother. *Come Be My Light: The Private Writings of the "Saint of Calcutta"*. Edited and with commentary by Brian Kolodiejchuk, M.C. New York: Doubleday, 2007.

Thérèse of Lisieux, Saint. Vol. 1 of *Sermon in a Sentence: A Treasure of Quotations on the Spiritual Life*, selected and arranged by John P. McClernon. San Francisco: Ignatius Press, 2002.

Weil, Simone. *Gravity and Grace*. Translated by Arthur Wills and arranged by Gustave Thibon. 1952. New York: Routledge, 2002.

———. *Waiting for God*. Translated by Emma Craufurd. 1951; New York: Routledge, 2010.